ScieNCe DictioNary

for kids

ScieNCE DictioNary
for kids

LAURIE E. WESTPHAL

PRUFROCK PRESS INC.
WACO, TEXAS

Library of Congress Cataloging-in-Publication Data

Westphal, Laurie E., 1967-
  Science dictionary for kids : the essential guide to science terms, concepts, and strategies /
Laurie E. Westphal.
      p. cm.
  Includes bibliographical references and index.
  ISBN-13: 978-1-59363-379-0 (pbk.)
  ISBN-10: 1-59363-379-3 (pbk.)
  1. Science--Dictionaries, Juvenile. I. Title.
  Q123.W47 2009
  503--dc22
                          2009016223

Copyright © 2009 Prufrock Press Inc.
Edited by Lacy Compton
Cover and Layout Design by Marjorie Parker

ISBN-13: 978-1-59363-379-0
ISBN-10: 1-59363-379-3

Printed in the United States of America.

At the time of this book's publication, all facts and figures cited are the most current avail-
able. All telephone numbers, addresses, and Web site URLs are accurate and active. All publi-
cations, organizations, Web sites, and other resources exist as described in the book, and all
have been verified. The author and Prufrock Press Inc. make no warranty or guarantee con-
cerning the information and materials given out by organizations or content found at Web
sites, and we are not responsible for any changes that occur after this book's publication. If
you find an error, please contact Prufrock Press Inc.

Prufrock Press Inc.
P.O. Box 8813
Waco, TX 76714-8813
Phone: (800) 998-2208
Fax: (800) 240-0333
http://www.prufrock.com

Dedication
Special thanks and lots of love to:
Ken and Irene Westphal, my mom and dad.
You have always been there for me,
excluding the backyard swing incident, of course.

Contents

Introduction

"Science is a way of thinking much more than it is a body of knowledge."—Carl Sagan

As Carl Sagan stated, the study of science is much more than just facts and knowledge; yet without the specialized vocabulary that accompanies the scientific concepts and processes, a person will find himself at a disadvantage as he strives to express himself scientifically. That is where *Science Dictionary for Kids* comes to the rescue.

This dictionary is much more than a list of words with dictionary definitions, although it does contain science words and, yes, definitions. The vocabulary used in science is vast; many of the words resemble commonly used words, however, their scientific usage may be very different. There also are many science words that are new and difficult for students to remember. These are the words that will be found in this dictionary, those new and seemingly difficult words or those that have significantly different definitions than common language. In addition to definitions of these specially chosen words written in everyday language (rather than dictionary language), readers also will find common examples and drawings for many of the words in order to create better understanding.

This book does not stop at vocabulary words commonly included in science dictionaries. Instead, it addresses other information that would be helpful to students on their way to becoming scientific thinkers. Readers also will find diagrams and graphics of the different cycles studied in the science classroom. The diagrams have the content presented in a basic way. It is not intended to replace instruction, rather to serve as an introduction or reminder of what was previously studied. It is meant to be user friendly, so if parents would like to have their children work ahead, or teachers would like their students to have a basic understanding of the content, these drawings will accomplish that. How many times do students read a definition or make a drawing before it is introduced and not understand what they have just drawn?

There also is a reference guide devoted to commonly used formulas and units used in science. Science is filled with standard units (e.g., kilograms and meters) and derived units (e.g., Newtons, which is a kilogram • meter, and a Joule, which equals a Newton • meter)—could it get any more confusing? Students can get more wrapped up in the units than the content when they do not remember with what each unit is associated. And, what about the multitude of formulas that exist in science? Students often have a formula sheet, but they have to manipulate or change the formulas in order to finish the problem. In this book's guide, students will be able to locate the target word, read its brief definition, and review the formula for its calculation (including units.)

In order to assist readers in moving beyond the "body of knowledge," this book contains many resources to help them be successful with their experiments in the laboratory. Although time often is taken to explain the proper names and uses for all of the scientific equipment at the beginning of the school year, by March students might have forgotten about the dangers of turning the eyedropper upside down to move liquids or have regressed to calling beakers "those cup things" again! This book has an entire section devoted to the equipment and glassware that students may work with in the science classroom, including a definition, but more importantly, a drawing (for easy identification) and if appropriate, specific directions for the equipment's use—such as how to transport liquid in an eyedropper without blowing air into the liquid and turning it upside down. What a time saver to not have to review *all* of the equipment the day of the experiment. It also is very effective to have students review the equipment on their own before it is used so if a review is needed, it is a very quick one on the day of the lab.

In addition to equipment, there also is a quick reference section to assist students with the various steps of the scientific method from creating testable questions to writing procedures and how to visibly present data through the creation of different types of graphs. Students can quickly flip to the instructions on multiple line graphs and be on their way to producing their own. These quick reference pages are meant to assist the reader in the steps of the scientific method in a quick, concise way.

From equipment usage to the steps of the scientific method, this book is much more than a standard dictionary. It is intended to assist teachers in reinforcing their content as well as parents who are willing to help their child understand a science concept. It is a ready reference to fill the gaps, bring ideas back to mind, and allow students to be even more self-sufficient in the scientific way of thinking.

Scientific Equipment

Anemometer
A weather instrument used to measure wind force and speed.

Barometer

A weather instrument used to measure atmospheric pressure. Below 29 is considered rainy or stormy while 30 or above is considered fair weather.

Beaker
A container used to transport, pour, or mix liquids. It cannot measure an exact amount of liquid.

Bunsen Burner

A small burner used in the laboratory. It is connected to a gas source and uses a very hot flame. When heating, the hottest area is at the top of the inner core.

Compass
An instrument used to find direction. It usually is made of a magnetic needle that is free to move until it is lined up with Earth's magnetic field.

Scientific Equipment

Compound Light Microscope

A light microscope that has more than one lens that is used to magnify a small object or specimen.

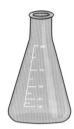

Erlenmeyer Flask

A flat-bottomed, cone-shaped flask used for mixing and heating liquid. A stopper can be used to seal it.

Eyedropper

A tube with a rubber bulb on the end that is used to pull liquid into the tube. It is used for transporting small amounts of liquid.

Eyewash

Safety equipment that is used to flush the eyes in case something gets into them during a lab experiment.

Funnel

A utensil used to pour small solids or liquids into small-mouthed containers. It is usually made of either plastic or glass.

Goggles

Safety equipment used to protect your eyes during an experiment.

Graduated Cylinder

A cylinder that has been marked with different "graduations," or lines and numbers, to show the level of the liquid put in it. Always read the meniscus, or the bottom of the curved liquid, when using a glass graduated cylinder.

Hand Lens

A hand-held magnifying glass that allows you to look closely at objects. The typical magnification is 10x; it makes the object 10 times bigger.

Hot Plate

A device used to heat beakers or flasks, it has either coils or a ceramic plate for heating. Always be sure the cord is tucked away for safety!

Hydrion Paper

A special kind of litmus paper that turns different colors depending on the pH (acidity or alkalinity) of the substance being tested.

Litmus Paper

Paper used to determine pH. The paper changes color depending on whether it has been put in an acid, base, or neutral substance. Red litmus paper will turn blue when placed in a base and blue litmus paper will turn red when placed in an acid.

Meniscus

The lowest part of the curve created by water when it is placed in a glass graduated cylinder. When reading the exact amount in a glass graduated cylinder, you look at where the meniscus lies.

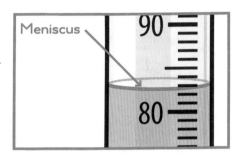

Meter Stick

A common instrument for measuring length in the classroom.

Pan Balance

A balance that uses two different pans to find the mass of an object.

Petri Dish

A shallow dish approximately 10 centimeters in diameter, used for growing bacteria cultures or evaporating crystals.

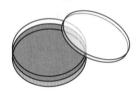

Ring Stand

A metal stand that usually includes a ring and is used to support glassware during heating or other lab equipment during an experiment.

Spring Scale

A measuring device or scale that uses a spring to measure the weight of an object. The most common unit measured using a spring scale is Newtons; 4.45 Newtons equals 1 pound.

Stopper

A cork or plug that is placed in glassware to seal it. It can be made of cork, plastic, or rubber and can either be solid or have holes in it to allow glass tubing to pass through.

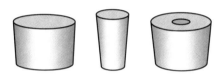

Stream Table

A long table that is used to show weathering, erosion, and water flow in streams and bodies of water.

Telescope

An instrument that uses lenses and mirrors to view faraway objects. There are three types: refracting, reflecting, and radio, which does not have any lenses or mirrors but depends on radio waves given off by faraway objects in space.

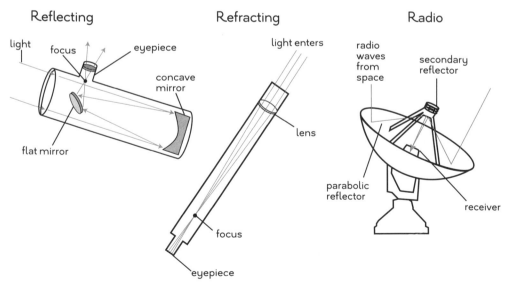

Scientific Equipment

Test Tube

A long glass tube that has one end open with the other end rounded. It can be used for heating, mixing, or collecting chemicals. Because it has a rounded bottom and cannot stand on its own, it usually needs to be kept in a rack.

Test Tube Clamp

A clamp designed specifically to hold test tubes while they are being heated. To open the clamp, squeeze the middle loops.

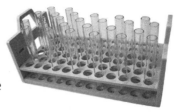

Test Tube Rack

A rack made out of wood or plastic specifically designed to hold test tubes while they are being used. Some also have a row of rods in the back on which to place the test tubes upside down for drying.

Thermometer

A device used to measure temperature. It contains mercury or colored alcohol, which expands and rises in the thermometer as the temperature increases. Thermometers measure temperatures in Celsius or Fahrenheit, or both. Some current thermometers provide digital readings.

Triple Beam Balance

A balance that is used to determine the mass of an object.

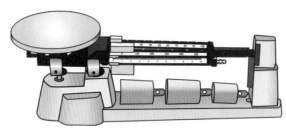

The Scientific Process

Bar Graph

A graph or chart that shows information using bars. It should be used to compare qualities of data.

Conclusion

A summarization of the results of the experiment and their impact on the hypothesis.

Control (Controlled Variables)

All of the aspects of an experiment that are kept constant and not changed. In a well-planned experiment, all of the factors should be controlled except the independent (manipulated) variable.

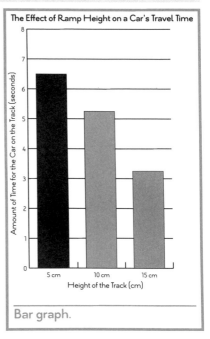

The Effect of Ramp Height on a Car's Travel Time

Bar graph.

Example: When testing how the height of a ramp affects the time it takes a car to go down it, the following are controlled: same ramp, same car, same timer, same person who takes the time, and same release technique of the car.

Control (Control Group)

When designing an experiment, this group or object remains as it is; no changes are made to it.

Data

A group of facts or measurements gathered either through research or experimentation.

Data Table

A table that is designed to record quantitative information gained in an experiment.

Dependent Variable

The outcome or results of the experiment; another name for the responding variable.

Example: When testing how the amount of sunlight affects the height of a bean plant, the height of the bean plant is the dependent variable.

Hypothesis

An educated guess or prediction (based on either research or previous experience) about the result of an experiment.

Examples: If a ramp is raised higher, it will take less time for a car to travel down it. Based on previous experiments, the bigger the wheels on the car, the faster it will travel.

Independent Variable

The variable that is changed in an experiment; another name for a manipulated variable.

Example: When testing how the amount of sunlight affects the height of a bean plant, the amount of sunlight is the independent variable.

Inference

Using an observation to come to a conclusion.

Example: In the picture we can observe a broken window and a baseball on the floor. Based on the observations, we could make an *inference* that the baseball broke the window.

Line Graph

A graph that shows information using lines; usually used to show data that were collected over time.

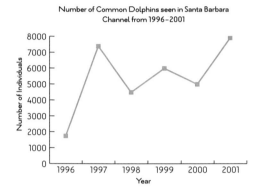

Manipulated Variable

The variable that is changed in an experiment; another name for an independent variable.

Example: When testing how the amount of sunlight affects the height of a bean plant, the amount of sunlight is the manipulated variable.

Observation

The act of gathering data by using one or more of the five senses.

Problem

The question to be considered and addressed in an experiment. The hypothesis usually answers this question.

Examples: How does the number of batteries affect the strength of the current in a circuit? Does water temperature affect the breathing rate of goldfish?

Procedure

The steps or plans that need to be followed to complete an experiment.

The Scientific Process

Qualitative Observations

Characteristics or qualities that describe what is being observed; based on a person's opinion. Do not involve numbers or measurements.

Examples: Color, texture, taste, likes or dislikes, comparisons (e.g., Stan is taller than me.)

Quantitative Observations

Observations that can be measured and recorded using quantities or numbers.

Examples: Mass, length, volume, number of something, recorded time

Responding Variable

The outcome of the experiment; another name for the dependent variable.

Example: When testing how the amount of sunlight affects the height of a bean plant, the height of the bean plant is the responding variable.

Scientific Method

A tool used by scientists to find the answer to a question or problem. The steps of the scientific method are:
1. Identify the Problem
2. Conduct Research
3. Create a Hypothesis
4. Perform an Experiment
5. Analyze the Data
6. Develop a Conclusion

Theory

A general principle or idea that explains facts or past events or that can be used to predict future events.

Trial

A test that is conducted more than once during an experiment.

Measurements and Units

Ampere (A)
The unit for electric current or the amount of electrons passing a point in a certain amount of time.

Astronomical Unit (AU)
The unit used to measure long distances in space. It is equal to the distance from the Earth to the sun.

1 AU = 149,597,870,691 km (149.60 x 10^9 km)

1 AU = 93 million miles (9.3 x 10^6 mi)

Calorie (cal)
A unit of energy; kilocalories (1,000 calories) are commonly used to describe the amount of energy found in food.

1,000 calories = 1 kilocalorie

1 calorie = 4.18 joules

Celsius (°C)
The metric temperature scale on which water freezes at 0° and boils at 100°.

Fahrenheit (°F)
The standard temperature scale at which water freezes at 32° and boils at 212°.

Gram (g)
The basic metric unit used to measure mass.

1 gram = 1,000 milligrams

1,000 grams = 1 kilogram

Gravity Constant (g_c)

The speed at which an object will accelerate as it falls toward Earth (until it reaches terminal velocity). It is also called the acceleration (due to gravity).

$g_c = 9.8 \text{ m/sec}^2$

Hertz (Hz)

The metric unit for frequency. It is the number of waves that pass a certain point in one second.

1 Hertz = 1 wave/second

Joule (J)

The metric unit for energy and heat.

1 joule = 1 Newton of force · 1 meter

1 joule = 1 watt/1 second

4.18 joules = 1 calorie

Kelvin (°K)

The temperature scale that begins at absolute zero, where there is no molecular movement. Water freezes at 273°K and boils at 373°K.

°Kelvin = °Celsius + 273

Light Year (ly)

The amount of distance light can travel through space in one year. It is used to measure long distances in space. A light year equals about 9.461 trillion (9.461×10^{12}) kilometers or 5.879 (5.879×10^{12}) trillion miles.

Example: Our nearest star is 4.4 light years away, so it takes light from that star 4.4 years to reach the Earth.

Measurements and Units

Liter (l)

A metric unit for volume.

1,000 liters = 1 cubic meter (m^3)

1 liter = 1,000 milliliters

1,000 liters = 1 kiloliter

Meter (m)

The basic metric unit of length.

1 meter = 1,000 millimeters

1 meter = 100 centimeters

1,000 meters = 1 kilometer

Newton (N)

The metric unit for force. It is equal to the amount of force needed to accelerate a mass of one kilogram at a rate of one meter per second per second.

1 Newton = 1 kg·m/s^2

4.45 Newtons = 1 pound

Ohm (Ω)

The metric unit for resistance.

1 ohm = 1 volt/1 ampere

Volt (V)

The standard metric unit for voltage or the force of electricity.

1 volt = 1 ohm · 1 ampere

Measurements and Units

Watts (W)

The standard metric unit for power. It is equal to one joule of energy per second.

1 watt = 1 joule/1 sec

1,000 watts = 1 kilowatt

1,000,000 watts = 1 megawatt

Measurements and Units

Life Sciences

Acquired Traits

Abilities that are helpful to an organism but are not passed on from a parent.

Example: Large arm muscles developed by training for a sporting event

Allele

A letter that represents a genetic trait and a member of a pair of genes on a chromosome. Written in pairs and used in Punnett Squares.

Amphibian

A cold-blooded vertebrate that is born under water, using its gills to breathe, then spends the rest of its life on land, using lungs to breathe.

Examples: Frogs, toads, newts, salamanders

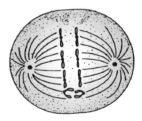

Anaphase

The stage of mitosis and meiosis when the chromosomes are separated from each other.

Anther

The part of the flower that produces and contains the pollen.

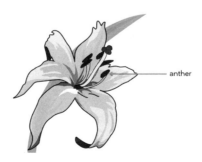

anther

Life Sciences

Biome

A large geographical area of the Earth's surface that has a certain set of characteristics.

Examples: Tundra, taiga, grassland, fresh water, salt water, deciduous forest, desert, tropical rainforest

Camouflage

An adaptation that helps an animal blend into its surrounding and helps it avoid predators.

Example: The arctic fox has white fur in the winter and brown fur in the summer.

Carbon (Dioxide) Cycle

The way in which carbon (in the form of carbon dioxide) is removed from the atmosphere by living things and ultimately returned to the atmosphere.

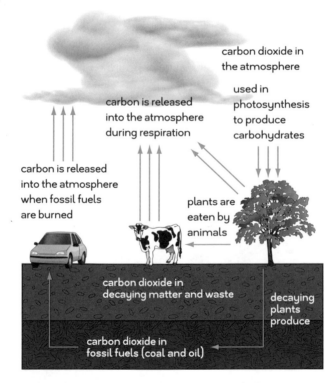

carbon dioxide in the atmosphere

used in photosynthesis to produce carbohydrates

carbon is released into the atmosphere during respiration

carbon is released into the atmosphere when fossil fuels are burned

plants are eaten by animals

carbon dioxide in decaying matter and waste

decaying plants produce

carbon dioxide in fossil fuels (coal and oil)

Life Sciences

Carnivore

Any living thing with a diet consisting mostly of meat.

Examples: Lion, venus flytrap, bear

Cell

The smallest functional unit of all living things.

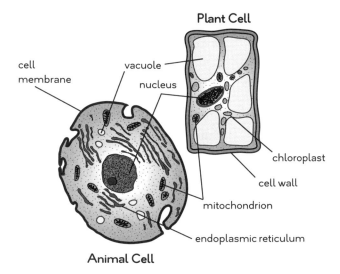

Cell Membrane

The barrier around a cell's cytoplasm (see cell).

Cold–Blooded

A living thing that cannot control its body temperature. Its temperature is determined by its environment.

Example: In order to get warm, a lizard or snake will lay on warm sand or in direct sunlight to bring up its body temperature.

Commensalism

A symbiotic relationship between organisms in which one of them benefits from the relationship and the other is not affected.

Example: Barnacles that attach themselves to whales (and ships)

Compound Light Microscope
A light microscope that is used to create an enlarged image of an object.

Consumer
An organism that feeds on plants or other animals.

Decomposer
An organism that breaks down dead animals and decaying matter into other substances.

Examples: Bacteria, fungi

Dichotomous Key
A key that allows you to identify an item based on a series of choices.

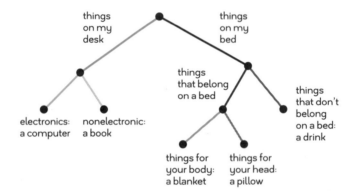

DNA (Deoxyribonucleic Acid)
The molecule that carries the genetic information in a cell. It has a "twisted ladder" or double helix shape.

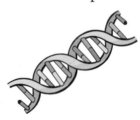

Dominant Trait

A trait that will appear in children (offspring) if one of the parents has the trait. It is written with a capital letter when writing the alleles for the traits in a Punnett square.

Example: Because tall is a dominant trait in pea plants, the tall trait would be written as T.

Endoplasmic Reticulum

A group of pathways in the cytoplasm of the cell that help move materials through the cell.

Epidermis

1. The outermost layer of the skin.
2. The outermost layer of a leaf.

Filament

The long tube-like structure that holds up the anther of a plant.

filament

Food Chain

The sequence of how living things eat each other in a biological community. It always starts with a primary energy source (usually the sun).

sun   producer   consumer   consumer   decomposer

Food Web

Two or more food chains interconnected together.

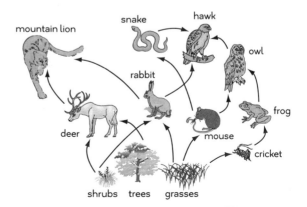

mountain lion   snake   hawk   owl   rabbit   frog   deer   mouse   cricket   shrubs   trees   grasses

Life Sciences

Fruit

The fleshy part of a plant that contains the seeds.

Examples: Tomato, apple, orange

Genotype

The genetic makeup of an organism as shown by the alleles or letters that represent the trait.

Example: The genotype for a heterogeneous tall pea plant would be: Tt.

Genotypic Ratio

The ratio of the genotypes of predicted offspring using a Punnett square.

Example: By using a Punnett square, you can calculate that the four possible offspring would be: TT, Tt, Tt, and tt. The genotypic ratio for this would be 1:2:1.

Golgi Apparatus

An organelle found in the cytoplasm of cells that processes and packages substances the cell needs.

Habitat

The area or environment where an organism normally lives or has its needs met.

Herbivore

An organism that depends on plants for most of its food and energy.

Heterozygous

When an organism has two different alleles for a genetic trait.

Examples: Tt is a heterozygous tall plant or Rr would be a heterozygous round seed.

Hibernation

A state of inactivity in which an organism conserves energy through the colder months.

Homozygous

When an organism has two of the same alleles for a genetic trait.

Examples: TT is a homozygous tall plant or tt would be a homozygous short plant.

Hybrid

Another term for having heterozygous alleles for a certain trait.

Examples: Tt is a hybrid or heterozygous tall plant, and Rr is a hybrid or heterozygous round seed.

Inherited Trait

Traits that come from a parent or other ancestor.

Examples: Eye or hair color

Instinct

A behavior that an organism is born with and does without thinking or training.

Example: Birds migrating south for the winter

Interphase

The phase of mitosis where the cell is resting. Growth and maturing are taking place during this phase.

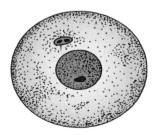

Life Sciences

Invertebrates

Animals that do not have a backbone.

Examples: Jellyfish, insect, spider, clam, starfish, ant

Learned Behavior

An action or set of actions that an organism learns and changes based on its experiences.

Examples: Tying your shoes, or when a cat comes to the sound of the can opener as a can of food is opened

Life Cycle

The life sequence of any organism as it passes from egg to adult.

Frog Life Cycle

Mammals

Animals that are warm-blooded, have body hair, and provide milk for their young. There are three groups: marsupials, monotremes, and placentals.

Examples: Kangaroo, elephant, anteater, bat

Marsupials

Mammals whose young stay in pouches for the first part of their life.

Examples: Koalas, kangaroos

Meiosis

The process of cell division in which a parent cell divides and produces four daughter cells (sex cells) that have half of the chromosomes of the parent.

Metaphase

The phase of mitosis where the chromosomes line up in the middle of the cell.

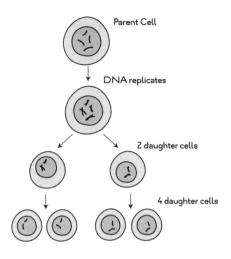

Parent Cell

DNA replicates

2 daughter cells

4 daughter cells

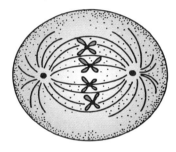

Mimicry

When one organism looks like another organism, helping it survive in its environment.

Example: The harmless scarlet king snake (red with yellow and black stripes, in which the red color is next to the black stripes) resembles the poisonous coral snake (red, black, and yellow stripes, but the red is next to the yellow stripes). Predators leave the scarlet king snake alone because it resembles the poisonous coral snake.

Mitochondria

An organelle found in the cytoplasm of cell that helps the cell convert food into useable energy.

Mitosis

The process of cell division in which a parent cell divides and produces two identical daughter cells, each with the same number of chromosomes as the parent cell.

Life Sciences

Monotremes

Mammals that lay eggs.

Examples: Anteaters, duck–billed platypus

Mutation

A permanent change in an organism's DNA.

Mutualism

A symbiotic relationship in which both organisms benefit from the relationship.

Example: Clown fish benefit from the protection of sea anemone, while the sea anemone benefit by eating the larger fish the clown fish attract as well as the clown fish's scraps.

Natural Selection

The idea that if an organism has characteristics or traits that help it survive better in its environment, it will survive to produce more offspring than other organisms that do not have the helpful trait. This will lead to the helpful trait becoming more and more evident in future generations.

Niche

The special area or function an organism has in its habitat.

Nitrogen Cycle

The steps by which nitrogen is taken out of soil and water by living things and ultimately returned back to the soil.

Nucleus

The control center for the cell that contains the genetic material, DNA.

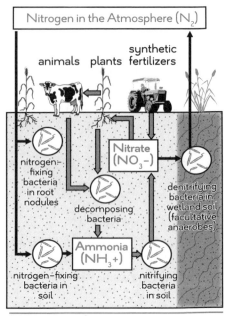

Nitrogen cycle.

Life Sciences

Omnivore

An organism that eats both plants and animals as its food source.

Organ

A part of an organism that performs a specific function.

Organelle

A structure in the cell that has a specific function.

Examples: Cell wall, cell membrane, nucleus, cytoplasm, nuclear membrane, endoplasmic reticulum, ribosome, mitochondrion, vacuole, lysosome, chloroplast

Organ System

A group of organs in the human body that work together to carry out a vital function.

Examples: Digestive, circulatory, respiratory, integumentary, endocrine, muscular, lymphatic, nervous, reproductive, skeletal, and excretory systems

Ovary

The part of a flowering plant that contains the seeds. It will mature into a fruit.

Parasitism

A symbiotic relationship in which one organism benefits from the relationship and the other organism is harmed.

Example: A dog and its fleas

Petals

The brightly colored parts of the flower that surround and help protect the reproductive parts of the flower.

petal

Life Sciences

Phenotype

The way an organism looks based on its genetic makeup or alleles.

Example: The phenotype for a plant with a genotype of Tt would be tall.

Phenotypic Ratio

The ratio of the phenotypes of predicted offspring using a Punnett square.

Example: By using a Punnett square, you can calculate that the four possible offspring would be: TT (tall), Tt (tall), Tt (tall), and tt (short). The phenotypic ratio for this would be 3:1, or 3 tall plants for every 1 short plant.

Phloem

The tissue in the stem of the plant that transports the food and nutrients throughout the plant.

Photosynthesis

The process in which plants use sunlight to combine carbon dioxide and water to create food. Its chemical formula is:

$$6 CO_2 + 6 H_2O + energy \longrightarrow$$
$$6 O_2 + C_6H_{12}O_6$$

carbon dioxide + water + sunlight $\longrightarrow$ oxygen + carbohydrate (sugar)

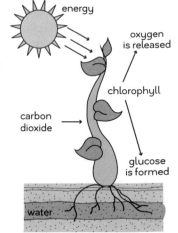

Pistil

The female reproductive parts of a flowering plant. It includes the stigma, style, and ovary.

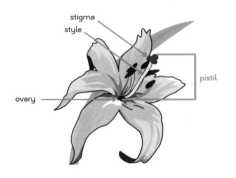

Prey
An animal that is hunted or caught for food.

Producer
An organism that produces its own food and is a food for other organisms; usually a green plant.

Prophase
The phase of mitosis where chromosomes copy themselves and the nucleus starts to disappear.

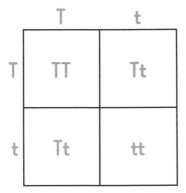

Punnett Square
A method used to predict the outcomes of genetic crosses.

	T	t
T	TT	Tt
t	Tt	tt

Purebred
Another term for having homozygous alleles for a certain trait.

Examples: TT is a purebred, or homozygous tall plant, or tt would be a purebred short plant.

Recessive Trait
A trait that has to be contributed by both parents in order to appear in the offspring. It will always be overridden by the dominant trait. Its allele is shown by using a lowercase letter.

Example: A short plant would have the genotype tt because tall is dominant (T).

Life Sciences

Reptiles

A group of cold-blooded animals that have scales, breathe air, and usually lay eggs.

Examples: Turtles, lizard, snakes, crocodiles, alligators

Respiration

The way that an organism exchanges gasses with its environment.

Ribosome

An organelle where protein synthesis takes place. It is found either in the cytoplasm of a cell or on an endoplasmic reticulum.

RNA (Ribonucleic Acid)

A long single strand of nucleic acid that assists a cell in making proteins.

Scavenger

An organism that feeds on dead or decaying animals.

Sepal

A modified leaf, sometimes looking like a petal, that is found at the base of the flower blossom.

Life Sciences

Stamen

The male reproductive parts of a flowering plant. It includes the anther and the filament.

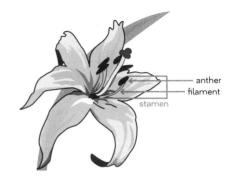

Stigma

The part of the female reproductive system in flowering plants that receives the pollen from the anthers. It is located at the top or end of the style.

Style

This female reproductive organ in flowering plants connects the stigma with the ovary.

Telephase

The phase of mitosis where the division between the two new cells forms.

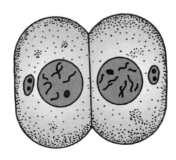

Life Sciences

Tissue

A group of similar cells that work together to perform a specific function for an organism.

Examples: Muscle, nerve, connective, epidermal

Trait

A feature or characteristic of an organism.

Transpiration

A process in plants in which they lose water through the undersides of their leaves.

Tropism

When an organism (usually a plant) moves toward or away from something.

Example: Plants grow toward sunlight or heat; hang a plant upside down and it will grow upright.

Vacuole

An organelle found in the cytoplasm of cells that is used to store water or nutrients. It usually is quite large in plant cells and smaller in animal cells.

Vertebrate

Animals that have a backbone.

Examples: Humans, dogs, horses, fish, reptiles, birds, amphibians, frogs

Warm-Blooded

An organism that can maintain a relatively constant body temperature no matter its environment.

Xylem

The tissue in the stem of the plant that transports water throughout the plant and helps support it.

Zygote

A cell formed from two cells—one from the mother and one from the father; the first cell of an offspring.

Physical Sciences

Acceleration

The amount velocity changes in a certain amount of time. Usually expressed in m/sec^2. A negative acceleration means the object is slowing down.

Calculating Acceleration:
- Use the formula: $A = \frac{V_f - V_i}{t}$
  - A = acceleration
  - V_f = the final velocity
  - V_i = the initial or starting velocity
  - t = the time for the acceleration to take place

Acid

A material that has a pH less than 7. It turns blue litmus paper red.

Examples: Citric acid (found in sodas and lemon juice), battery acid

Atom

The smallest piece of an element. Made up of a nucleus and a cloud of electrons.

Atomic Mass

The total mass of an atom; the number of protons and neutrons in an atom. Shown by the unit u, or the unified atomic mass unit.

Example: Silver's atomic mass is 107.87 u.

Atomic Number

The number of protons in an atomic nucleus.

Base

A material that has a pH greater than 7. It turns red litmus paper blue.

Examples: Baking soda, drain cleaner

Bohr Model

A model that shows the approximate location of the protons, neutrons, and electrons in an atom, with the electrons traveling in orbits around the nucleus.

Bohr Model of Chlorine

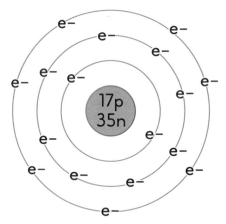

Boiling Point

The temperature at which a liquid boils. Water boils at 100°C or 212°F.

Buoyancy

The capacity to float in either air or liquid. The principal of buoyancy, which states that in order for an object to float it has to displace enough of the fluid around it, is attributed to Archimedes.

Chemical Change (Chemical Reaction)

Any change that creates a new substance by altering the chemical makeup of a compound. Evidence of a chemical change could be change in temperature, light, heat, or sound given off, or the formation of gasses.

Examples: Combustion (wood burning), oxidation (iron rusting), cooking (or baking)

Chemical Property

A property of a substance that can be observed during a chemical change.

Example: Combustibility (ability to burn), reactivity (with other elements)

Circuit

A closed path that electricity follows. There are two basic types: series and parallel.

Combustibility

How easily a material will ignite or burn. It also is a chemical property.

Compound

A substance made up of two or more elements that cannot be separated by a physical change.

Examples: Salt (NaCl), water (H_2O), sugar ($C_{12}H_{22}O_{11}$)

Conductivity

The ability of an object to conduct or transmit heat, electricity, or sound.

Conductor

A material that can allow heat, light, sound, or electricity to pass through it easily.

Example: Metal is a good conductor of heat and electricity because it transmits them so easily.

Current

The rate of flow of electrons (electric charges) or water. Electric current is measured in Amperes (A).

Calculating Current Given the Resistance:

- Use Ohm's Law formula: $I = \dfrac{V}{R}$
  - I = current (amps)
  - V = voltage (volts)
  - R = resistance (ohms Ω)

Calculating Current Given the Power:

- Use Ohm's Law formula: $I = \dfrac{P}{V}$
  - I = current (amps)
  - P = power (watts)
  - V = voltage (volts)

Density

A measure of the compactness of the molecules of a material. The closer the particles are to one another, the higher the density of the material. The mass per unit of volume of a material.

Calculating Density:

- Use the formula: $D = \dfrac{m}{v}$
  - D = density
  - m = mass
  - v = volume

Diatomic Molecule

A molecule that is made up of two atoms. It always will be bonded with another atom, even it is more of the same kind of atom.

Examples: Hydrogen (H_2), Oxygen (O_2), Fluorine (F_2), Iodine (I_2), Bromine (Br_2), Chlorine (Cl_2), Nitrogen (N_2)

Diffract/Diffraction

The bending of waves around an obstacle or the spreading of waves as they go through an opening.

Doppler Effect/Doppler Shift

When the frequency of a light or sound wave is changed because the object producing the wave is in motion. In sound, the higher the frequency, the higher the pitch; in light, the higher frequency light is blue while the lower frequency light is red.

Example: As an ambulance with its sirens blaring approaches you, the sound waves in front of it are compressed, giving it a higher frequency and therefore a higher pitch. As it passes you, the waves spread out so the frequency is lower and the pitch is lower as well.

Element

A substance made up of all of the same atoms. Found on the periodic table.

Electrons

Tiny negatively charged participles that move around the nucleus of the atom. Their mass is about $\frac{1}{1836}$ of a proton or neutron so they do not calculate into the atomic mass.

Calculating the Number of Electrons in an Atom:

- In an electrically stable atom, the number of electrons equals the number of protons (atomic number).

- Hydrogen has an atomic number of 1, which means it has one proton and one electron.

Electromagnet

Wrapped wire around an iron core that acts like a magnet when electric current flows through the wire.

Energy

The ability to do work. Measured in joules.

Families

The vertical columns of the periodic table; also called groups. Families have certain common characteristics or traits. There are 18 families in the standard periodic table.

Examples: Alkali metals, Alkaline Earth metals, halogens, noble gasses

Force

A push or a pull.

Frequency

The amount of waves that pass a certain point in one second. It is measured in Hertz (Hz).

Calculating Frequency:

• Use the formula: $F = \dfrac{v}{\lambda}$

  • F = frequency (Hertz)

  • v = speed (usually in m/sec)

  • λ = wavelength (in meters)

Friction

A force that resists motion when two objects move against each other.

Gas

A state of matter that does not have a definite shape or volume. It will fill the container in which it is placed. The particles have high energy and are in motion.

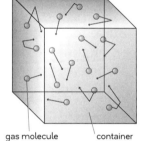

gas molecule   container

Gravity

A natural force of attraction between bodies in space with great mass and other objects in space as well as the objects on their surfaces. Gravity determines weight. Acceleration due to gravity: 9.8 m/sec^2

Groups

The vertical columns of the periodic table; also called families. Groups have common characteristics or traits. There are 18 groups in the standard periodic table.

Examples: Alkali metals, Alkaline Earth metals, halogens, noble gasses

Physical Sciences

Half-Life

The amount of time it takes for half of a radioactive material to decay.

Amount of Time Passed	Percentage of Original Amount That Is Still Present
0 half-lives	100%
1 half-life	50%
2 half-lives	25%
3 half-lives	12.5%
4 half-lives	6.25%
5 half-lives	3.125%
6 half-lives	1.5625%

Heterogeneous Mixture

A mixture in which the materials are different sizes and often different states of matter. It is easy to tell the difference between the different components in the mixture.

Examples: Cereal and milk, chicken noodle soup, snack mix, nuts and bolts

Homogenous Mixture

A mixture in which the different materials appear to be the same state of matter. The particles of the materials in the mixture are similar sizes so the different materials are difficult to tell apart.

Examples: Powered drinks in water, salt water, bronze

Inclined Plane

A simple machine consisting of a sloped surface or ramp used to raise a load.

Calculating the Mechanical Advantage (MA) of an Inclined Plane:

- Use the formula: $\dfrac{\text{Distance}_{effort}}{\text{Distance}_{resistance}}$

  - Distance_{effort} = length of the ramp
  - $\text{Distance}_{resistance}$ = height of the ramp

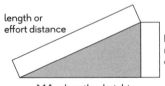

length or effort distance

height or resistance distance

MA = length ÷ height

Indicator

Any substance that can show the presence or absence of a chemical or substance.

Examples: Litmus paper (acids or bases), Hydrion paper (pH)

Inertia (Newton's First Law of Motion)

The tendency of a body to resist changing its motion. An object at rest will tend to remain at rest, while an object in motion will tend to remain in motion in a straight line unless acted upon by an outside force.

Examples: A soccer ball will continue on a straight path toward the goal unless blocked. A large rock at the top of a hill will remain where it is unless gravity acts upon it to pull it down.

Insoluble

A substance that cannot be dissolved in another substance.

Insulator

Material that slows down or does not allow the passing of heat, light, sound, or electricity.

Example: Rubber is a good insulator for both electricity and heat.

Ion

An atom or group of atoms that has acquired a charge because it has gained or lost electrons.

Example: A hydrogen atom has one proton (one positive charge) and one electron (one negative charge). This makes the atom electrically neutral. When hydrogen loses an electron, it loses one negative so that gives it a total charge of 1 positive. It is a +1 ion.

Isotope

Two atoms that have the same atomic number but different mass numbers, and therefore different numbers of neutrons. It is usually expressed with the element name and its mass (e.g., Carbon–14), and it may be radioactive.

Examples:
- Carbon–12 (its mass matches the periodic table)
    - Atomic Number = 6, so it has 6 protons
    - Atomic Mass = 12, so it has 6 neutrons
- Carbon–14 (it has a mass of 14—does not match the mass written on the periodic table)
    - Atomic Number = 6, so it has 6 protons
    - Atomic Mass = 14, so it has 8 neutrons
- Carbon–14 is an isotope of carbon.

Law of Conservation of Energy

A principle that states that energy is neither lost nor gained in any system or energy transfer.

Law of Conservation of Mass

A principle that states that mass is neither lost nor gained in any chemical reaction.

Lever

A simple machine made up of a bar that pivots around a fixed point.

Calculating Mechanical Advantage of a Lever
- Use the formula: $\dfrac{\text{Distance}_{\text{force or effort}}}{\text{Distance}_{\text{load or resistance}}}$
    - $\text{Distance}_{\text{force or effort}}$ = measure of the length from the force to the fulcrum
    - $\text{Distance}_{\text{load or resistance}}$ = measure of the length from the fulcrum to the load

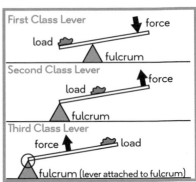

Liquid

A state of matter with a definite volume but no definite shape. It takes the shape of its container. Its molecules have energy and roll past each other.

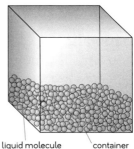

liquid molecule   container

Longitudinal (Compressional) Wave

A wave that travels parallel through its medium. The closer the particles of the medium, the faster the longitudinal wave can travel through it.

Examples: Sound waves, earthquake waves

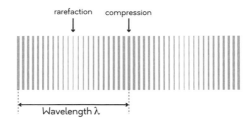

rarefaction   compression

Wavelength λ

Mass

The amount of matter inside an object. It does not change based on gravity. It is usually measured in grams or kilograms.

Matter

Something that has mass and takes up space. It can be solid, liquid, gas, or plasma.

Mechanical Advantage (MA)

The number of times a machine multiplies the force applied to it.

Calculating Mechanical Advantage:

• Use the formula: $MA = \dfrac{\text{Resistance Force}}{\text{Effort Force}}$

Melting Point

The temperature at which a solid changes to a liquid. Ice (water) melts at 0 °C or 32 °F.

Metalloid
An element on the periodic table that has properties of both metals and nonmetals. Located along the stairstep separating the metals from the nonmetals.

5 **B** 10.811 Boron	6 **C** 12.0107 Carbon	7 **N** 14.0067 Nitrogen	8 **O** 15.9994 Oxygen
13 **Al** 26.9815386 Aluminum	14 **Si** 28.0855 Silicon	15 **P** 30.973762 Phosphorus	16 **S** 32.065 Sulfur
31 **Ga** 69.723 Gallium	32 **Ge** 72.64 Germanium	33 **As** 74.92160 Arsenic	34 **Se** 78.96 Selenium
49 **In** 114.818 Indium	50 **Sn** 118.710 Tin	51 **Sb** 121.760 Antimony	52 **Te** 127.60 Tellurium
81 **Tl** 204.3833 Thallium	82 **Pb** 207.2 Lead	83 **Bi** 208.98040 Bismuth	84 **Po** [209] Polonium

Metalloids.

Metals
Substances found on the left side of the periodic table. They usually are good conductors of heat and energy.

Mixture
A combination of one or more substances in which each component retains its own properties and still can be separated. There are two types: heterogeneous mixtures and homogenous mixtures.

Examples: Cereal and milk, salad, powdered drinks, snack mix

Molecule
Consisting of two or more atoms joined together, it is the smallest particle of a substance that still has all of the properties of the substance.

Example: Water molecule is H_2O, with two atoms of hydrogen and one atom of oxygen.

Momentum
The amount of motion of a moving object.

Calculating Momentum:
- Use the formula: p = mv
  - p = momentum (kg • m/sec)
  - m = mass (kg)
  - v = velocity (m/sec)

Neutral

1. An atom or particle that does not carry a charge.
2. A solution that has a pH of 7. Pure water is a neutral substance.

Neutron

A neutral particle found in the nucleus of the atom. It has an approximate mass of 1 unified atomic mass unit.

Calculating the Number of Neutrons in an Atom:

1. Find the atomic mass (found on the periodic table) of an atom; it is equal to number of protons and neutrons together.

2. Calculate the number of neutrons by subtracting the number of protons (atomic number) from the atomic mass.

Example: Lithium has an atomic mass of 6.9 or 7. Based on its atomic number, it has 3 protons. Lithium has 4 neutrons.

Newton's First Law of Motion

An object at rest will remain at rest unless acted upon by an outside force; an object will continue to travel in a straight line unless acted upon by an outside force. Also called the Law of Inertia.

Example: When riding in a car, if the car suddenly stops, a rider not wearing a seat belt will continue moving at the speed of the car.

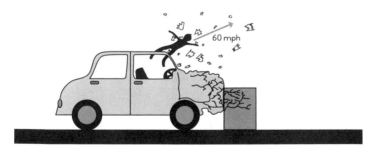

Newton's Laws of Motion

Three laws that show the relationships between forces acting on an object and the motion of the body.

Newton's Second Law of Motion

In order for an object to accelerate or move in the direction of the force placed upon it, you have to have enough force to overcome its mass.

Example: The more mass in the car, the more force it will take to move it. The faster you want it to move, the more force you will need.

Newton's Third Law of Motion

For every action, there is an equal and opposite reaction.

Example: In order for a rocket to leave the ground, hot gasses have to push downward while the rocket moves up.

Nonmetals

Substances found on the right side of the periodic table. They generally are not good conductors of heat and energy and most are gasses at room temperature.

Nucleus

The central part of an atom that contains the protons and neutrons.

Parallel Circuit

An electric circuit that has more than one path for the current to follow. If one light bulb (or resistor) is turned off or breaks, the current will follow the other path.

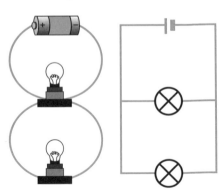

Particle

A very small piece or part of a substance or object.

Pendulum

An object suspended from a fixed point so it can swing (or oscillate) freely back and forth.

Calculating the Period of a Pendulum:
- Using a stopwatch, measure the amount of time it takes for the pendulum to make one complete swing out and return to its starting point.

Period

1. A horizontal row on the periodic table.
2. Time needed for one complete swing out and back to a pendulum.

pH (Potential of Hydrogen)

A measure of how acidic or basic a solution; 7 is considered neutral, while 1–6 are acidic and 8–14 are basic. The further away from neutral, the stronger the acid or base. See page 121 for a list of common acids and bases.

Phase

Another term for state of matter. There are four phases of matter: solid, liquid, gas, and plasma.

Physical Change

A change in size, shape, or state of matter that does not change a substance's composition.

Examples: Water melting or freezing, crumpling a piece of paper, liquid evaporating, breaking glass

Physics

The study of matter, energy, and force.

Pitch

How high or low a sound is. It is determined by the frequency. The higher the frequency (amount of waves in a second), the higher the pitch. The lower the frequency, the lower the pitch.

Plasma

1. A very hot, gas-like state of matter that occurs naturally on the sun and other stars. It also can be produced in fluorescent lights and plasma display televisions.
2. The liquid part of blood.

Power

1. The rate at which work is done. Measured in watts.

Calculating Power (Work):

- Use the formula: $P = \dfrac{W}{t}$

    - P = power (watts)
    - W = work (joules)
    - t = time (seconds, minutes, hours)

2. The amount of electricity being used. Measured in watts.

Calculating Power (Electricity):
- Use the formula: $P = V \cdot I$

    - P = power (watts)
    - V = voltage (volts)
    - I = current (amps)

Product

The substance or substances that are formed in a chemical reaction.

Property

Characteristics of an object or substance.

Examples: Chemical properties (flammability), physical properties (density)

Protons

Positively charged particles that are located in the nucleus of the atom. They have an atomic mass of 1 u.

Calculating the Number of Protons in an Atom:
- In an electrically stable atom, the element's atomic number equals the number of protons.

Example: Hydrogen has an atomic number of 1, which means it has just one proton.

Pulley

A simple machine made up of a grooved wheel that can turn freely in a frame called a block. There are two basic kinds: fixed (the pulley doesn't move) and moveable (the pulley moves along the rope). In addition, a block and tackle pulley is made of more than one pulley working together.

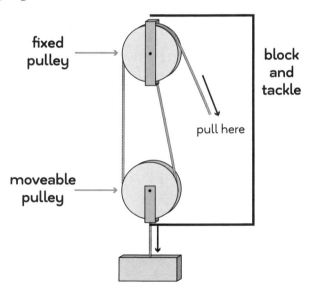

fixed pulley

block and tackle

pull here

moveable pulley

Reactant

A substance that is participating in a chemical reaction.

Reflect (Reflection)

To throw or bend back light or sound when it hits a surface.

Examples: Mirrors reflect light, echoes are reflected sound

Refract (Refraction)

To bend light as it passes through a material or lens or from one state of matter to another.

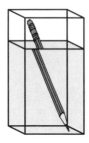

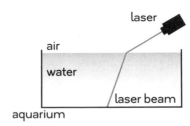

laser

air

water

laser beam

aquarium

Resistance

A measure of how much a material slows down or stops electricity. Measured in ohms.

Examples: Rubber has higher resistance so it is a poor conductor of electricity. Copper has low resistance so it is a good conductor of electricity.

Calculating Resistance:

- Use the formula: $R = \dfrac{V}{I}$
  - R = resistance (ohms Ω)
  - V = voltage (volts)
  - I = current (amps)

Saturated Solution

A solution that has dissolved all of a substance that it is able to dissolve at a certain temperature.

Screw

An inclined plane wrapped around a cylinder core.

Examples: Car jack, c–clamp, corkscrew

Series Circuit

An electric circuit that has only one path for the current to follow. If one light bulb (or resistor) is turned off or breaks, the path is broken and the current will stop.

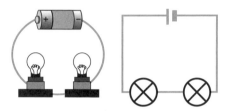

Simple Machine

A device without moving parts that is used to make work easier. There are six different kinds: lever, wheel and axle, pulley, wedge, inclined plane, and screw.

Solid

A state of matter with a definite shape and volume. Its particles have the lowest energy of all of the states of matter.

Solubility

The amount of substance or solute that can be dissolved in a certain amount of solvent.

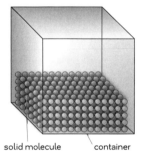

solid molecule   container

Solubility Graph

A graph that shows the relationship between temperature and the amount of a certain solute that can be dissolved in water.

Soluble

Able to be dissolved into another substance.

Solute

A substance that is being dissolved into something else.

Example: In making a powered drink, the powder is the solute.

Solution

A homogenous mixture of two or more substances; can be solids, gasses, or liquids.

Example: Air (solution of various gasses), soda (solution of gas in a liquid), bronze (solid solution of copper and tin)

Solvent

The substance into which something is being dissolved.

Example: In salt water, the solvent is water.

Speed

The rate of motion of an object. It is represented by the distance over the time an object travels.

Calculating Speed:

- Use the formula: $S = \dfrac{d}{t}$
  - S = speed
  - d = distance
  - t = time

Supersaturated Solution

A solution that has more substance dissolved in it than it would normally be able to have dissolved at a certain temperature.

Example: Heating and stirring water to dissolve sugar for sugar rock candy. If you just heated the water, it would not be able to dissolve as much as when it is stirred as well.

Temperature

Measure of the kinetic energy or motion of the molecules of a substance. It is expressed in Celsius, Fahrenheit, or Kelvin.

Calculating Celsius When Given Fahrenheit:
- Use the formula: $°C = (5/9)(°F - 32)$

Calculating Fahrenheit When Given Celsius:
- Use the formula: $°F = (1.8 \times °C) + 32$

Calculating Kelvin When Given Celsius:
- Use the formula: $°K = °C + 273$

Transverse Wave

A wave that travels at a 90° angle to the medium it is moving through.

Examples: Water waves, light waves

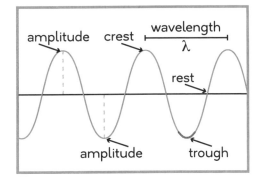

Unsaturated Solution

A solution that can still have more of a certain substance dissolved it in.

Valence Electrons

The electrons located in the outermost electron shell of an atom. They are the electrons involved in chemical reactions.

Example: Oxygen has two rings of electrons; the innermost one has two electrons. The second, or outermost, ring has six. These are the valence electrons. Oxygen has six valence electrons.

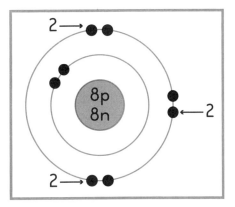

Voltage

The strength or force of the electrons or electrical current in a circuit. Technically, voltage is the difference of potential energy between two points of an electrical circuit. A good analogy is comparing electricity to water. High voltage is like water that is coming out of a power washer versus water that is coming out of a garden hose (lower voltage)

Example: High voltage signs warn that the current traveling through the circuit has a lot of energy and strength and could be dangerous.

Calculating Voltage Using Resistance:
- Use the formula: $V = IR$
  - V = voltage (volts)
  - I = current (amps)
  - R = resistance (ohms Ω)

Calculating Voltage Using Power:
- Use the formula: $V = \dfrac{P}{I}$
  - V = voltage (volts)
  - P = power (watts)
  - I = current (amps)

Volume

The amount of space an object occupies. Usually measured in L, mL, or cm^3 using a graduated cylinder.

Wavelength

The distance between two crests or two troughs in a transverse wave or the length of one compression and one rarefaction in a compressional wave.

Calculating the Wavelength:
- Use the formula: $\lambda = \dfrac{v}{F}$
  - λ = wavelength (in meters)
  - F = frequency (Hertz)
  - v = speed (usually in m/sec)

Wedge

A simple machine with an inclined plane on one or both sides.

Examples: Knife, axe, nail

Weight

A measure of how much gravity pulls on an object. It is measured using a scale and is expressed in Newtons.

Wheel and Axle

A large wheel secured to a smaller wheel or shaft called an axle.

Examples: Door knob, screwdriver, steering wheel

Calculating the Mechanical Advantage of a Wheel and Axle:
• Measure the radius of the wheel and divide by the radius of the axle.

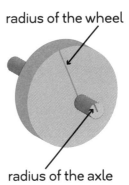

radius of the wheel

radius of the axle

Work

A force acting through a distance.

Calculating Work:
• Use the formula: $W = F \cdot d$
    • W = work (joules)
    • F = force (Newtons)
    • d = distance (meters)

Earth Sciences

Abrasion

The process of wearing away of rock by particles carried by wind, water, or ice.

Example: Rocks in the bottom of a glacier rub or scrape the bedrock as the glacier moves over it.

Asthenosphere

A relatively thin layer of the Earth, located in the upper part of the mantle, on which the Earth's plates rest and move.

Biomass

Plant material, animal waste, or vegetation that is used as a fuel or energy source.

Example: Wood, manure, yard clippings

Biosphere

The part of the Earth and its atmosphere that supports life.

Cementation

The last step in the formation of some sedimentary rocks. Minerals seep into the cracks between the sediments and cement them together.

Chemical Weathering

A form of weathering in which rocks and minerals are transformed into new substances.

Example: A rock with iron in it will react with the oxygen in the air and the rock will begin to "rust" and break off.

Cirrus
A high altitude cloud, having a thin white and wispy appearance.

Cleavage
A line or plane that a rock will break along naturally.

Compaction
The compressing of rock and sediments that can form sedimentary rocks.

Condensation
When water vapor changes into liquid. In the water cycle, this step leads to precipitation.

Conduction
The transfer of heat or electricity by direct contact.

Example: The handle of a metal spoon gets hot when it is left in a pot of boiling water.

Continental Drift
The theory that the continents are able to move and drift freely on the surface of the Earth; usually credited to Alfred Wegener.

Convection

A heat transfer through liquids and gasses. Also known as convection currents.

Convergent Boundary

A place where two or more plates come together.

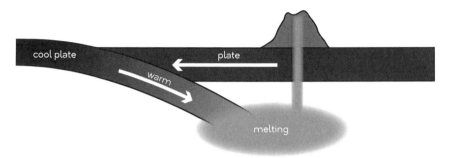

Core

The innermost part of the Earth. It is composed of an iron and nickel liquid outer core and a solid iron inner core.

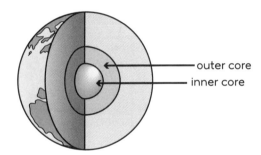

Crust

The outermost layer of the Earth's surface. It is broken into large pieces called plates, ranging from approximately 3 miles (5 km) to 47 miles (75 km) in thickness.

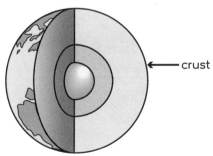

Cumulus

A dense, fluffy white cloud with a flat base and rounded top.

Delta

A fan-shaped landform formed at the mouth of a river as the river slows down and sediments are deposited.

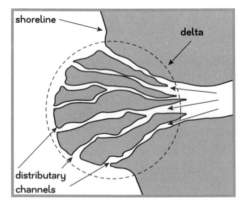

Deposition

The dropping of material that has been picked up and transported by wind, water, or ice.

Divergent Boundary

A boundary in which two plates are moving away from each other.

Example: The Mid-Atlantic Ridge found in the center of the Atlantic Ocean

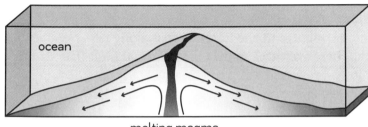

melting magma

Epicenter

The point on the Earth's surface that is directly above the focus of an earthquake.

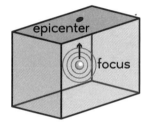

Era

The longest division of geologic time.

Examples: Precambrian, Paleozoic, Mesozoic, Cenozoic

Erosion

The process of moving soil and rock by water, wind, or glacial action.

Evaporation

The process in the water cycle in which water from the oceans and lakes is heated up enough by the sun to turn into water vapor in the atmosphere.

Exosphere

The uppermost region of the Earth's atmosphere; where the atmosphere mixes with space.

Extrusive

Igneous rocks that are formed from lava above the Earth's surface. Usually have very small or no crystals.

Examples: Pumice, obsidian, basalt

Fault (Fault Line)

A crack or fracture in the Earth's crust along which movement occurs. There are three main types: normal fault (the hanging wall slips down), reverse fault (the hanging wall is pushed up), and slip strike (the pieces of crust move past one another).

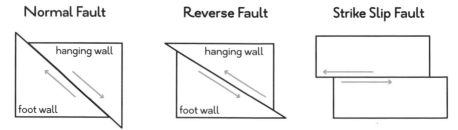

Fission

A nuclear reaction in which an atomic nucleus is split into fragments, releasing a significant amount of energy.

Focus

The exact location where the crust moved, causing an earthquake.

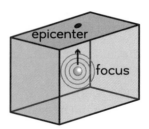

Fold

A bend in the layers of rock.

Foliated

A rock that has a layered appearance. This is usually associated with metamorphic rocks.

Fusion

A nuclear reaction in which smaller atomic nuclei are brought together to form a larger nuclei, releasing energy. This occurs naturally in stars and our sun.

Generator

A machine that converts mechanical energy (energy in motion) to electrical energy.

Geothermal (Hydrothermal) Energy

Using the heat from within the Earth to create energy. Hydrothermal energy is specifically using the hot steam in the Earth's crust.

Glacier

A large river of ice slowly flowing over a landmass as its mass and gravity forces it forward. Although it stays year-round, it will move forward or recede based on the snowfall and temperatures.

Half-Life

The amount of time it takes for half of a radioactive material to decay.

Amount of Time Passed	Percentage of Original Amount That Is Still Present
0 half-lives	100%
1 half-life	50%
2 half-lives	25%
3 half-lives	12.5%
4 half-lives	6.25%
5 half-lives	3.125%
6 half-lives	1.5625%

Humus

The organic part of soil. Usually dark in color, it is created by the decomposition of living material.

Earth Sciences

Igneous Rock

A rock formed from molten material, either at or below the Earth's surface.

Examples: Pumice, basalt, granite, obsidian

Inexhaustible Resource

A natural resource that will not be exhausted or consumed completely.

Examples: Solar energy, wind energy

Intrusive

Igneous rocks that are formed from magma below the Earth's surface. Usually have larger crystals.

Examples: Granite, diorite, gabbro

Lava

Molten rock at or above the Earth's surface.

Lithosphere

The strong outer layer of the Earth that is divided into 12 major plates and many more smaller ones.

Luster

A description of the surface of a crystal, rock, or mineral.

Examples: Metallic, nonmetallic, dull

Magma

Molten rock below the Earth's surface; contains dissolved gasses.

Mantle

The middle layer of the Earth. Although considered solid, it can move. Comprises most of the Earth's mass.

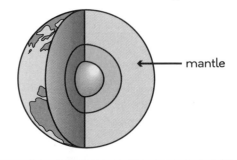

Meander

A bend in a river formed by erosion and deposition along its banks. It can eventually be cut off and turn into an oxbow lake.

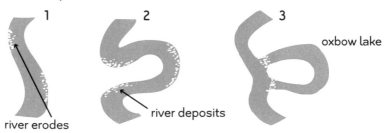

Mesosphere

The middle layer of the Earth's atmosphere. Temperatures decrease in this layer as altitude is increased.

Metamorphic Rock

A rock formed by heat and pressure deep within the Earth's crust.

Examples: Slate, gneiss, marble

Meteorologist

A scientist who predicts and reports weather conditions.

Mineral

A naturally occurring solid that has a definite chemical composition, color, hardness, and crystalline structure.

Examples: Diamond, quartz, gold, silver

Moraine

An accumulation of the sediments left behind by a glacier.

Nonrenewable Resource

A natural resource that cannot be restored after use or is being used at such a rate that it cannot be replaced as quickly as it is being consumed.

Examples: Oil, natural gas, petroleum

Ore

A mineral that can be mined for profit.

Examples: Aluminum, iron, copper

Pangaea

The name of a supercontinent that is believed to have existed before the continents drifted apart. Proposed by Alfred Wegener as part of the theory of continental drift.

Period

The division of geologic time into which eras are divided.

Examples: The Mesozoic Era is divided into the Cretaceous, Jurassic, and Triassic periods.

Permeability

The ability of a material to transmit fluids. An aquifer must have permeable rock for the water to move through it.

Physical or Mechanical Weathering

The process of breaking down rocks into smaller fragments using physical means.

Example: Ice wedging (water gets into cracks in rocks and freezes, breaking the rock apart)

Plate Tectonics

The theory that the crust of the Earth is broken into large pieces called plates that are being pushed and moved through convection currents in the Earth's mantle.

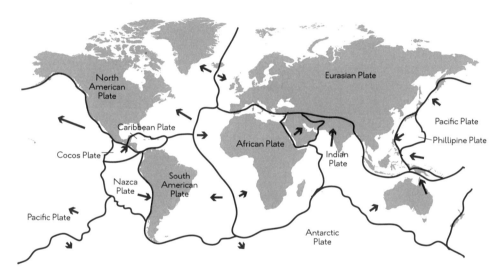

Precipitation

Any form of water that falls to the Earth's surface.

Examples: Rain, snow, sleet, hail

Radiation

A transfer of energy that does not require matter to take place.

Examples: Sunlight, heat lamps

Renewable Resource

A natural resource that can be replenished at the current rate it is currently being consumed by humans.

Examples: Fresh water, wood, biomass, geothermal power

Rock Cycle

The sequence of events that shows how rocks are initially formed and changed over time.

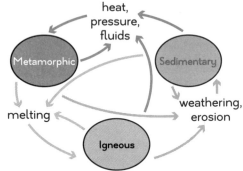

Runoff

Water that is not absorbed by rocks or soil so it flows over the ground.

Sedimentary Rock

A rock formed by the compaction or cementation of layers of sediment being laid down on top of each other.

Examples: Coal, limestone, conglomerate, shale

Sediments

Weathered materials that have been carried and deposited by wind, water, or ice.

Seismograph

An instrument that detects and records the intensity, direction, and duration of an earthquake.

Solar Power

An inexhaustible energy source in which the energy of the sun is captured and converted into useful types of energy. The energy usually is captured with large solar panels located in direct sunlight.

Stratosphere

The layer of the atmosphere immediately above the troposphere. It contains the ozone layer.

Stratus

A grey cloud with layers that is close to the ground.

Example: Fog

Streak

The color of the powder left behind when a mineral is rubbed against a hard surface (usually a streak plate).

Subduction Zone

An area where one edge of a crustal plate is forced below another plate; associated with a convergent plate boundary.

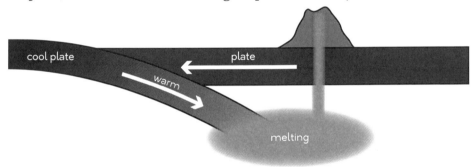

Thermosphere

The layer of the Earth's atmosphere directly beneath the exosphere. Temperatures increase in this layer as altitude is increased.

Tidal Power

Energy created by ocean waves that is captured and used to turn a turbine.

Topographic Map

A map that is a two-dimensional representation of a three-dimensional land surface. These maps show the size, shape, and elevation of various land features.

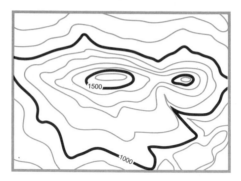

Transform Boundary

A boundary in which two plates are passing beside each other.

Example: San Andreas Fault

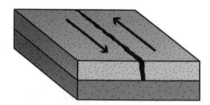

Troposphere

The layer of the atmosphere that is closest to the surface of the Earth. Clouds and weather are found in this layer.

Tsunami

A huge wave that is caused when the waves from an underwater earthquake travel through the water. As the waves get closer to shore, they begin to pile up until they smash on shore.

Water Cycle

The cycle that shows how water is transferred and changed from the bodies of water into the atmosphere and then back to the ocean.

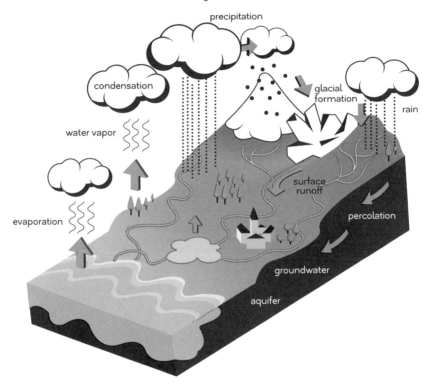

Weather Map Symbols

Symbols or letters used on a weather map to show the current weather. A complete list is included in the quick reference guide on page 124.

Common symbols:

- ●●● Warm Front
- ▼▼▼ Cold Front
- ▲▼▲ Stationary Front
- :• Rain
- ✳ Snow

- ○ Fair, No Clouds
- ◑ Partly Cloudy
- ● Overcast

Weathering

The process of breaking down rock into smaller pieces and sediments. There are two types: physical and chemical.

Wind Power

A renewable energy source in which the energy of wind is captured and converted into useful types of energy. Usually captured with large wind turbines located in areas of constant wind.

Space Sciences

Asteroid

Any of the rocks or bodies in space that revolve around the sun, usually located between Mars and Jupiter.

Black Hole

An area in space with such strong gravitational pull that even light cannot escape its pull.

Comet

A body in space that travels in a long orbit around the sun. It is made up a solid head with a long vapor tail that always points away from the sun.

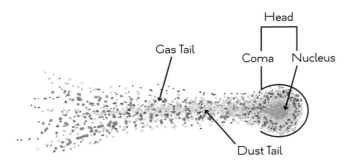

Examples: Halley's Comet (appears every 76 years) and Hale–Bopp (appears every 2,400 years)

Constellation

A formation of stars that seem to form pictures in the night sky.

Examples: Cassiopeia, Orion, Cygnus, the astrological signs

Corona

The plasma-like atmosphere of the sun. It is what is visible during a total solar eclipse.

Crescent

One of the phases of the moon, associated with the coming (waxing) or going (waning) of the new moon.

Waning Crescent   Waxing Crescent

Eclipse

When a body in space is either partially or completely blocked from sight.

Lunar

• Occurs when the Earth's shadow falls on the moon, blocking it from sight. Occurs about every 6 months.

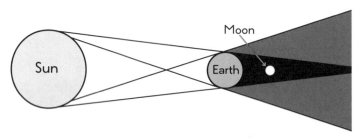

Solar

• Occurs when the moon passes directly between the Earth and sun, so the sun is blocked from view. Usually lasts less than 8 minutes.

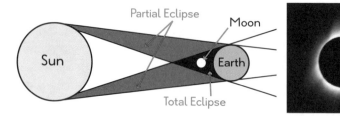

Elliptical Galaxy

A galaxy with no spiral structure that seems to have an elliptical shape, containing mostly older stars.

Examples: Messier 32, Messier 87, Leo I

Image Credit: NASA, ESA, and the Hubble Heritage (STScI/AURA)–ESA/Hubble Collaboration

Full Moon

The phase of the moon when it is directly behind the Earth and completely lit by the sun's light.

Galaxy

A large group of stars, dust, gas, and other bodies held together by gravity. They are classified by their shapes. There are three main types: elliptical, spiral, and irregular.

Spiral Galaxy
(Milky Way)

Elliptical Galaxy

Irregular Galaxy

Image Credit: NASA/courtesy of nasaimages.org

Image Credit: NASA, ESA, and the Hubble Heritage (STScI/AURA)–ESA/Hubble Collaboration

Image Credit: NASA, ESA, the Hubble Heritage Team (STScI/AURA), and A. Aloisi (STScI/ESA)

Gibbous

The moon's phases in which more than half of the moon's surface is visible.

Waning Gibbous   Waxing Gibbous

Irregular Galaxy

A galaxy that has a unique shape and is not symmetrical. Comprised of both young and older stars, it is the least common shape for galaxies.

Examples: Large Magellanic Cloud, Messier Objects

Image Credit: NASA, ESA, the Hubble Heritage Team (STScI/AURA), and A. Aloisi (STScI/ESA)

Light Year

The amount of distance light can travel through space in one year. It is used to measure long distances in space. A light year equals about 9.46 trillion (9.46×10^{12}) kilometers or 5.88 (5.88×10^{12}) trillion miles.

Example: Our nearest star is 4.4 light years away, so it takes light from that star 4.4 years to reach the Earth.

Meteorite

A rock or piece of metal that has fallen to Earth's surface from space.

Moon or Lunar Phases

The change in the appearance of the moon to an observer on Earth as the moon revolves around the Earth. See page 125 of the quick reference guide for a full lunar phase chart.

Nebula

A large cloud of space dust or gasses.

New Moon

A phase of the moon in which the moon is between the sun and the Earth so the side facing the Earth does not receive any sunlight.

New Moon

Orbit

The path an object follows when it goes around another object.

Example: The moon orbits the Earth.

Prominence

An arc of flaming gas erupting from the sun's surface.

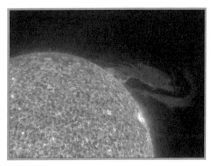

Image Credit: NASA

Protostar

A tightly packed cloud of material that is in the process of becoming a star.

Quarter

The phase of the moon in which half of the illuminated side of the moon is visible to Earth.

First Quarter Last Quarter

Radio Telescope

A telescope that collects radio waves given off by bodies in space. The radio waves then are translated into photographs based on the types of radio waves received. Scientists cannot look through radio telescopes.

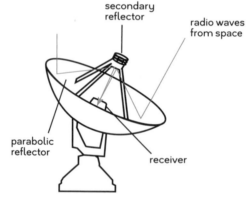

secondary reflector

radio waves from space

parabolic reflector

receiver

Reflecting Telescope

A telescope in which light for a faraway object is gathered, reflected, and focused by mirrors before being passed through the eyepiece to the observer.

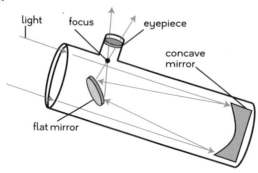

light   focus   eyepiece

concave mirror

flat mirror

Space Sciences

Refracting Telescope

A telescope in which light from a faraway object is gathered and focused by various lenses before being magnified one more time as it passes through the eyepiece lens to the observer.

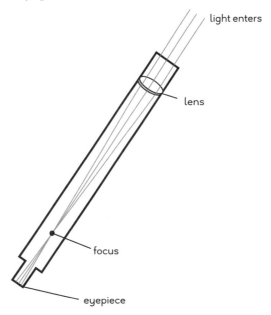

Revolution

The movement of a body around another in space. The Earth revolves around the sun, which accounts for our seasons. 1 orbit = 1 year.

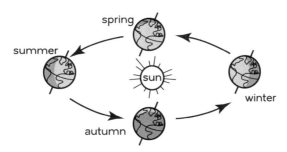

Rotation

The turning on a center point or axis. The Earth's rotation on its axis causes day and night. 1 rotation = 1 day.

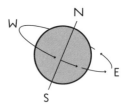

Satellite

A body in space that orbits a planet. It can be natural like a moon or man-made.

Solar Flare

A sudden eruption of hydrogen gas on the surface of the sun; appears as a very bright spot. It usually occurs near sunspots.

Spiral Galaxy

A galaxy that has arms that seem to "spiral" out from a compacted center. Made up of mostly young bright stars.

Examples: Milky Way Galaxy, Pinwheel Galaxy

Image Credit: NASA/courtesy of nasaimages.org

Sun Spot

Cool, dark spots that appear on the sun's surface.

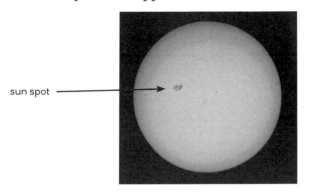

sun spot

Supernova

The explosion of a star that gives off lots of light and energy.

White Dwarf

The remains of a star after it has collapsed. Its particles are very tightly packed and it does not give off much light. It is near the end of the cycle of a star.

Space Sciences

Quick Reference Guide

Using Lab Equipment

Using a Microscope

1. Plug in the microscope and be sure the cord is tucked safely out of the way.
2. Move the objective lenses so the lowest power (the shortest lens) is pointing down toward the stage.
3. Place the slide on the microscope stage, putting it under the stage clips to keep it from moving. Be sure the specimen is over the middle of the hole in the stage. That will make it easier to find, but don't look yet!
4. Looking at the objective lenses, use the coarse focus (bigger knob) and move the lens to its lowest point, closest to the slide.
5. Look through the eyepiece and slowly turn the coarse focus until the specimen comes into focus.
6. Once it is in sight, if needed, adjust the fine focus to see more details.
7. If the specimen seems washed out or hard to see, adjust the diaphragm to allow *less* light to pass through the hole in the stage. This will bring out more detail.

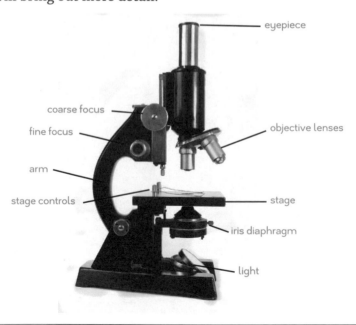

- eyepiece
- coarse focus
- fine focus
- arm
- stage controls
- objective lenses
- stage
- iris diaphragm
- light

Using a Triple Beam Balance

1. Be sure the balance is zeroed, or measures zero, when there is nothing being massed. The balance indicator (usually a line on the right) should be lined up showing it's balanced. Different balances have different ways of zeroing them.
2. Place the object to be massed on the pan of the balance.
3. Starting with the largest (heaviest slider), move the slider into each notch along the beam until the balance indicator goes below the balance line.
4. Return the slider to the last notch it was in before it went too low.
5. Using the next smallest slider, move it from notch to notch until the balance indicator again goes below the balance line.
6. Return the slider to the last notch it was in.
7. Use the last slider (usually a small metal one without notches), and slide it slowly along the beam until the balance indicator and balance line match exactly.
8. Add the different numbers indicated on each beam to calculate the mass.

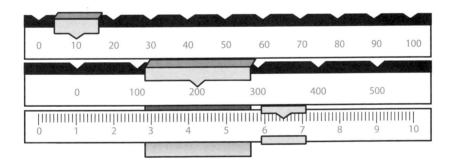

These beams read 10, 200, and 6.5, so the mass is 10 + 200 + 6.5, or 216.5 grams.

Using a Spring Scale

1. Be sure your scale is "tared," or measuring zero, when nothing is being weighed.
2. Attach the object to be weighed to the scale.
3. To measure the weight of the object, lift the object off the table using the scale.
4. To measure the force it takes to move an object, pull the object along the table or ground with the scale.

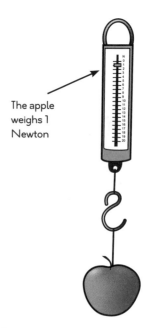

The apple weighs 1 Newton

Using a Pan Balance

1. Place the objects you want to mass in one of the pans.
2. Place masses (or weights) in the other pan until the pans balance. There usually is a line or pointer that needs to be matched up to show exact balance.
3. Count the masses (or weights) that were put in the second pan to determine the mass of the object.

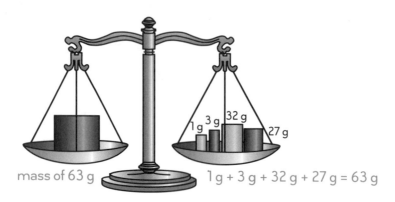

mass of 63 g   1 g + 3 g + 32 g + 27 g = 63 g

Using an Eyedropper

1. Squeeze the bulb at the top of the eyedropper.
2. Place the eyedropper into the liquid you want to transport.
3. Slowly release the bulb at the top to draw liquid into the eyedropper.
4. Without tipping or turning the eyedropper upside down, move it to the new location and slowly squeeze the bulb at the top to release the liquid one drop at a time.

Reading a Graduated Cylinder

1. Be sure the graduated cylinder is on a flat surface.
2. Look at the curved level of the liquid in the cylinder. The curved surface is called a meniscus.
3. The lowest point of the meniscus is the volume of the liquid.

Note: Plastic graduated cylinders do not create meniscuses.

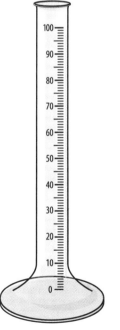

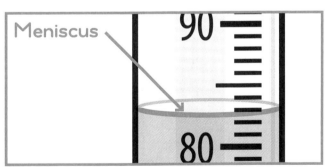

Meniscus

Measuring Volume

Measuring the volume of a regular solid:

1. Measure the length, width, and height of the object using a meter stick or ruler.
2. Multiply the measurements to get the volume.

Measuring the volume of an irregular solid:

1. Fill a graduated cylinder with water to a certain level.
2. Read the meniscus and record the volume of the water.
3. Add the solid to the graduated cylinder.
4. Record the new volume after the solid was added.
5. Subtract the two volumes to calculate the volume of the solid.

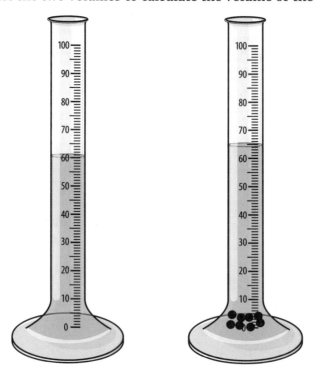

The initial volume in this cylinder was 60 ml. After the solid was added, it went up to 65 ml. The change was 5 ml, so that is the volume of the solid.

Measuring the Density of an Object
1. Find the mass of the object using a balance.
2. Find the volume of the object, either through measurement and calculation or through displacement using a graduated cylinder.
3. Divide the mass by the volume.

Example: According to a triple beam balance, a rock has a mass of 56 grams. After putting it in a graduated cylinder and using displacement, the volume is 10 ml. The density is 5.6 g/ml or 56 grams/10 ml.

The Scientific Method

Steps of the Scientific Method
1. Identify the Problem
    a. Decide on a testable question that can be answered through experimentation.

2. Conduct Research
    a. Collect background information on the problem and the topic being studied.
    b. Find out what others already know about the topic and problem.

3. Create a Hypothesis
    a. Propose a solution to the problem based on the research and previous knowledge.

4. Perform an Experiment
    a. Test your hypothesis and collect the data.

5. Analyze the Data
    a. Organize, examine, and graph the data obtained through the experiment.

6. Develop a Conclusion
    a. Summarize the results of the experiment and its impact on the hypothesis.

Developing an Appropriate or Testable Question

The problem being investigated has a question that needs to be answered. This question needs to be testable in order to gather information and approach your problem.

To be sure your question or problem is testable, ask yourself these questions:
1. Can it be answered through an experiment?
2. Can you make observations in order to answer the question?
3. Does it compare two things that can be measured?
4. Can you obtain quantitative data (using measurements) to answer this question?
5. Does it ask about objects, organisms, or events in the natural world?

Nontestable Questions
1. Depend on personal preference or moral values.
2. Ask about the supernatural.
3. Relate to ideas that cannot be measured.

Testable Questions	Nontestable Questions
Do vegetarians experience more heart attacks than meat eaters?	Is vegetarianism better than eating meat?
What if I added one more battery to a parallel circuit?	What is inside a battery?
How does temperature affect evaporation?	How do the seasons affect dogs?
How does soil type affect plant growth?	Which soil type is better?
What features of a parachute affect the time it takes to fall?	How does building height affect a parachute?

Tips for Writing Specific Procedures
1. Include a materials list with everything needed to complete the experiment.
2. Write the procedures step-by-step; do not leave anything out!
3. Number each step.
4. Make steps short, to the point, and easy to understand.
5. Include specific measurements as well as exact names of the equipment (e.g., 250 mL beaker rather than large cup).
6. Include a drawing or sketch to show how the experiment is set up if it will help.
7. Include any safety rules or cautions.
8. If possible, have another person read through your procedures to see if anything was left out.

Common Lab Safety Rules

1. Follow all written and verbal instructions carefully.
2. Do not work in the lab without a teacher present.
3. Wear safety goggles when instructed. Keep them on during the entire experiment, even if you or your lab group is already finished.
4. Conduct yourself in a responsible way at all times.
5. Only perform the experiment given or approved by your teacher.
6. Do not touch, smell, or taste any chemicals unless your teacher tells you to do so.
7. Always carry microscopes, triple beam balances, and glassware with chemicals using two hands.
8. Report an accident (breakage, spill, etc.) or injury to the teacher immediately.
9. Do not pick up broken glass or clean up any chemical spills.
10. Know where all of the safety equipment is located and how to use it.
11. Be sure the cords on any equipment are safely stored where they cannot be pulled or tripped over.
12. Never leave an open flame or hot plate unattended and never assume a hot plate is not hot.
13. Do not eat food, drink beverages, or chew gum.
14. Keep your hands away from your face, eyes, and mouth while using lab materials. Always wash your hands after an experiment.
15. Do not use or play with any equipment, supplies, or other materials in the science room without permission from the teacher.
16. Tie long hair back when working with equipment.
17. Treat any preserved biological specimens with respect.
18. Keep your work area neat and clean and clean all work areas and equipment at the end of the experiment.
19. Always dispose of any waste materials as instructed. Do not return unused chemicals to their original containers.

Collecting and Recording Your Data

Creating a Data Table

1. Identify the independent and dependent variables.
2. Decide on a title for your data table that tells the purpose of the data table.
3. Write your independent variable (what you are going to change and how) in the first column. Don't forget your units!
4. Make columns to record all of the details about your dependent variable (or results).
5. If appropriate, make more than one column for the dependent variable so more than one trial can be recorded.
6. If using more than one trial, include a column to calculate the average of the results.

Title

Independent Variable	Dependent Variable			Average of the Trials
	Trial 1	Trial 2	Trial 3	

The Effect of Ramp Height on Car's Travel Time

Height of Ramp (cm)	Time of Car on Track (sec)			Average of the Trials
	Trial 1	Trial 2	Trial 3	
5 cm	6.4 sec	6.2 sec	6.9 sec	6.5 sec
10 cm	5.2 sec	5.0 sec	4.8 sec	5.0 sec
15 cm	3.2 sec	3.5 sec	3.3 sec	3.3 sec

Graphing Your Data

Creating a Bar Graph From a Data Table

The Effect of Ramp Height on Car's Travel Time

Height of Ramp (cm)	Time of Car on Track (sec)			Average of the Trials
	Trial 1	Trial 2	Trial 3	
5 cm	6.4 sec	6.2 sec	6.9 sec	6.5 sec
10 cm	5.2 sec	5.0 sec	4.8 sec	5.0 sec
15 cm	3.2 sec	3.5 sec	3.3 sec	3.3 sec

1. Identify the independent (what was changed in the experiment) and dependent (measured results of the change) variables.

    Independent = height of the ramp (centimeters)

    Dependent = time of car on track (seconds)

2. Label each axis with its variable. Be sure to include units if they are needed.

    Independent variable on the horizontal (x) axis

    Dependent variable on the vertical (y) axis

3. Determine the range of the data for each variable by subtracting the largest number from the smallest number needed on each axis.

    Height of ramp (x axis) = 15 cm – 0 cm = 15

    Time of car (y axis) = 6.5 sec – 0 sec = 6.5

4. Count the number of lines on each axis of your graph.

    15 lines on each axis

Quick Reference Guide

5. Divide the range for the y axis by the number of lines on your graph. This is will give you the value for each line on the y axis.

   Time of car on track (y axis) = 6.5 sec/15 lines = .43 sec/line (round to .5 sec/line)

6. Count the number of independent variables in the experiment to determine the number of bars.

   Heights: 5, 10, and 15, so 3 bars.

7. Decide how to place the bars (equally spaced) on the x axis.
8. Number the lines of your graph.
9. Use the data to create bars that show your quantities.

   (5, 6.5) (10, 5.0) (15, 3.3)

10. Give the graph a meaningful title.

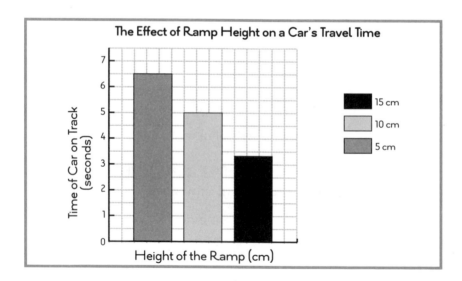

Quick Reference Guide

Creating a Line Graph Using Data From a Data Table

The Effect of a Heat Lamp on the Evaporation of Water

Number of Days Passed	Amount of Water Left (mL)			Average of the Trials
	Trial 1	Trial 2	Trial 3	
0	90 ml	90 ml	90 ml	90 ml
1	71 ml	72 ml	67 ml	70 ml
2	58 ml	58 ml	52 ml	56 ml
3	42 ml	46 ml	38 ml	42 ml
4	23 ml	27 ml	19 ml	23 ml
5	6 ml	8 ml	4 ml	6 ml

1. Identify the independent (what was changed in the experiment) and dependent (measured results of the change) variables.

   Independent = number of days passed

   Dependent = amount of water left (mL)

2. Label each axis with its variable. Be sure to include units if they are needed.

   Independent variable on the horizontal (x) axis

   Dependent variable on the vertical (y) axis

3. Determine the range of the data for each variable by subtracting the largest number from the smallest number needed on each axis.

   Number of days (x axis) = 5 days – 0 days = 5

   Amount of water left (y axis) = 90 mL – 0 ml = 90

4. Count the number of lines on each axis of your graph.

   15 lines on each axis

5. Divide the range for each axis by the number of lines on your graph. This will give you the value for each line. Round your answers if you need to make it easier to plot your information.

Amount of water left (y axis) = 90 mL/15 lines = 6 mL/line

Number of days (x axis) = 5 days/15 lines = .33 days/line (use three lines for 1 day)

6. Number the lines of your graph.
7. Plot the data on your graph and connect the points.

(0, 90) (1, 70) (2, 56) (3, 42) (4, 23) (5, 6)

8. Give the graph a meaningful title.

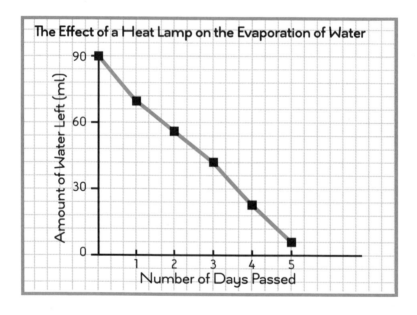

Creating a Multiple Line Graph

The Evaporation Rate in Different Spots in Our School

Number of Days Passed	Amount of Water Left		
	Under a Heat Lamp	Dark Closet	On the Classroom Table
0	15 ml	15 ml	15 ml
1	6.4 ml	15 ml	10 ml
2	0 ml	13.5 ml	6 ml
3	0 ml	12 ml	3 ml
4	0 ml	11 ml	0 ml
5	0 ml	9 ml	0 ml

1. Identify the independent (what was changed in the experiment) and dependent (measured results of the change) variables.

   Independent = time (days)

   Dependent = amount of water left (ml)

2. Label each axis with its variable. Be sure and include units if they are needed.

   Independent variable on the horizontal (x) axis.

   Dependent variable on the vertical (y) axis.

3. Determine the range of the data for each variable by subtracting the largest number from the smallest number needed on each axis.

   Number of days (x axis) = 5 days – 0 days = 5

   Amount of water left (y axis) = 15 ml – 0 ml = 15

4. Count the number of lines on each axis of your graph.

   15 lines on each axis

5. Divide the range for each axis by the number of lines on your graph. (This will give you the value for each line.) Round your answers if you need to make it easier to plot your information.

   Amount of water left (y axis) = 15 ml/15 lines = 1 ml/line

   Number of days (x axis) = 4 days/15 lines = .27 sec/line
   (round to .3 sec/line)

6. Number the lines of your graph.
7. Make a key for each of the sets of information that will be put on the graph and place it near your graph.

   heat lamp

   classroom table

   dark closet

8. Plot the data on your graph for each line and connect the points using the key to show each line.

   Heat lamp = (0, 15) (1, 6.4) (2, 0) (3, 0) (4, 0) (5, 0)

   Dark closet = (0, 15) (1, 15) (2, 13.5) (3, 12) (4, 11) (5, 9)

   Classroom table = (0, 15) (1, 10) (2, 6) (3, 3) (4, 0) (5, 0)

9. Give the graph a meaningful title.

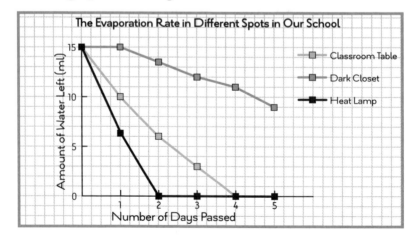

Atoms

Calculating the Number of Protons
The number of protons is equal to the atomic number of the element.

>Fluorine's atomic number is 9 = 9 protons

Calculating the Number of Neutrons
The number of neutrons is equal to the atomic mass minus the atomic number.

>Fluorine has a mass of 18.9 (round to 19) – 9 (atomic number) = 10 neutrons

Calculating the Number of Electrons
In a stable atom, the number of electrons is equal to the number of protons, which is equal to the atomic number.

>Fluorine has 9 protons = 9 electrons

Creating a Basic Bohr Model for an Element With an Atomic Number Between 1–20
1. Calculate the number of protons, neutrons, and electrons in the atom.
2. Place the protons and neutrons in the nucleus of your model.
3. After calculating the number of electrons, place them in their electron rings.

>1st Ring = 2 electrons
>
>2nd Ring = 8 electrons
>
>3rd Ring = 8 electrons
>
>4th Ring = 4 electrons

Determining if an Atom Is an Ion or an Isotope

1. Calculate the number of protons, neutrons, and electrons based on the periodic table.

   Example: Fluorine has 9 protons, 10 neutrons, and 9 electrons.

2. Compare the number of each particle in your question atom with the numbers you just calculated.

3. If the number of neutrons are different, it is an **isotope**.

   Example: Fluorine with 9 protons, 11 neutrons, and 9 electrons is an isotope. The number of neutrons is different from the one calculated based on the periodic table.

4. If the number of electrons is different, it is an **ion.**

   Example: Fluorine with 9 protons, 10 neutrons, and 10 electrons is an ion. The number of electrons is different from the one calculated from the periodic table.

Determining the Charge of an Ion

1. Using the periodic table, calculate the number of electrons for the atom.

   Example: According to the periodic table, Calcium should have 20 electrons.

2. Compare the number of electrons in your atom with what was calculated.

   Example: Our Calcium ion has 18 electrons, which is two less than the periodic table calculation.

3. If there are fewer electrons that what is stated on the table, your ion is positive by the difference.

   Because Calcium has 18 electrons, which is two less than the table, it is a positive 2 or 2+ ion.

4. If there are more electrons than what is stated on the table, your ion is negative by the difference.

> Example: If a Chlorine atom had 18 electrons, which is one more than is calculated from the table. That means the ion is negative by one or a 1 – ion.

Genetics

Creating and Completing Punnett Squares

Punnett squares are used to predict the genetic outcome of the offspring that may be produced when two organisms are bred together or "crossed."

1. Carefully read the given information for the cross.

   Complete a cross between a homozygous (purebred) short pea plant and a heterozygous (hybrid) tall pea plant.

2. Determine which trait is dominant (will always show if present) and which is recessive (will only show if no dominant trait is present).

   In pea plants, tall is dominant over short.

3. Designate letters for the trait or genes in the cross.

   Capital letters represent dominant traits, and lowercase letters represent recessive traits.

   T = tall plants

   t = short plants

4. Locate the important words in the cross to help you identify the makeup of each parent.

   homozygous or purebred = the plant has two of the same alleles (or letters) for this trait; so either TT (dominant) or tt (recessive)

   heterozygous or hybrid = the plant has different alleles for this trait; Tt

5. Using the information given, write the genotype (genes) for each parent.

   homozygous (purebred) short = tt

   heterozygous (hybrid) tall = Tt

   So: tt x Tt (Read as tt crossed with Tt)

6. List the genes that each parent can contribute to the cross.

   tt will contribute a t and a t

   Tt can contribute a T and a t

7. Draw a Punnett square and write the possible contributions from one parent along the top, and the other along the side.

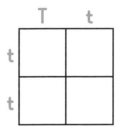

8. Fill in each box by writing the trait that is both above and beside it.

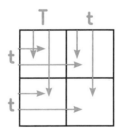

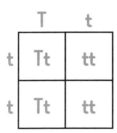

Determining the Genotypic Ratio From a Punnett Square

1. Complete your Punnett Square. The letters inside the square represent the genotype or genetic makeup of the offspring.

   Tt and tt in the example below.

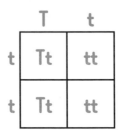

2. Count the number of each genotype.

   Tt = 2

   tt = 2

3. Write down and reduce the ratio of each genotype produced in the cross.

   Tt to tt

   2 to 2 or reduces to 1:1.

   So its genotypic ratio is 1:1. For every plant that has genotype of Tt, there should be one with tt as its genotype.

Determining the Phenotypic Ratio From a Punnett Square

1. After completing your Punnett Square, write the phenotype of physical appearance of each offspring in its square.

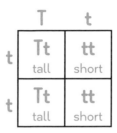

Remember: Because a capital letter is the dominant trait, if there is at least one capital letter, the offspring will have that trait.

2. Count the number of each phenotype.

Tall plants = 2

short plants = 2

3. Write down and reduce the ratio of each genotype produced in the cross.

Tt to tt

2 to 2 or 1:1. Therefore, its phenotypic ratio is 1:1. For every short plant, there should be one tall one!

4. Note: The genotypic and phenotypic ratios are **not always** the same!

Quick Reference Guide

Solubility Curves

Reading a Solubility Graph

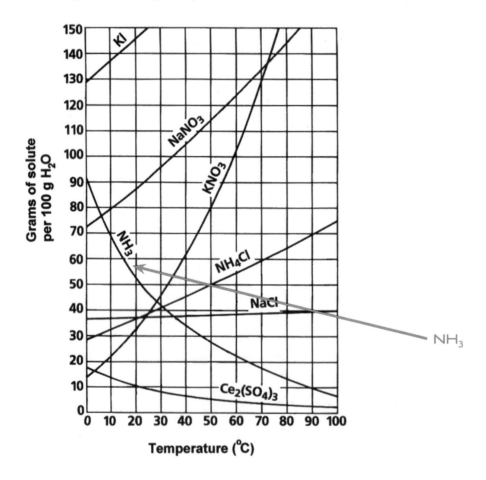

1. Locate the curve for the substance being dissolved. Ignore all of the other curves!

    Let's use the NH_3 curve.

2. To create a saturated solution, the curve will show the exact amount of grams of the substance that can be dissolved in 100 grams of water at any temperature 0°C – 100°C.

   For example, look at the curve and find 10°C for NH_3. The curve shows 70 grams of NH_3 will create a saturated solution in 100 grams of water.

Determining the Solubility of a Solution

1. Locate the correct curve for the substance being dissolved.
2. Find the intersection of the amount of substance and the temperature of the water.
3. If the intersection of the two is below the curve for the substance, it is considered an unsaturated solution.

   For the temperature 10°C, if there is 50 grams of NH_3 dissolved in the 100 grams of water, the solution is unsaturated.

4. If the intersection of the two is above the curve for the substance, it is considered a supersaturated solution.

   For the same temperature, if there are 90 grams of NH_3 dissolved in the 100 grams of water, then the solution is supersaturated.

Formulas

Motion

	Formula	Definition of Terms
Speed	$S=\dfrac{d}{t}$	S = speed d = distance t = time
Acceleration	$A=\dfrac{V_f-V_i}{t}$	A = acceleration V_f = the final velocity V_i = the initial or starting velocity t = the time for the acceleration to take place
Momentum	$p = mv$	p = momentum (kg · m/sec) m = mass (kg) v = velocity (m/sec)

Density

	Formula	Definition of Terms
Density	$D=\dfrac{m}{v}$	D = density m = mass v = volume

Temperature

	Formula	Definition of Terms
Celsius	$°C = (5/9)(°F - 32)$	°C = degrees Celsius °F = degrees Fahrenheit
Fahrenheit	$°F = (1.8 × °C) + 32$	°F = degrees Fahrenheit °C = degrees Celsius

Current

	Formula	Definition of Terms
Current	$I = \dfrac{P}{V}$	I = current (amps) P = power (watts) V = voltage (volts)
Current	$I = \dfrac{V}{R}$	I = current (amps) V = voltage (volts) R = resistance (ohms Ω)
Voltage	$V = I \cdot R$	V = voltage (volts) I = current (amps) R = resistance (ohms Ω)
Resistance	$R = \dfrac{V}{I}$	R = resistance (ohms Ω) V = voltage (volts) I = current (amps)
Power	$P = V \cdot I$	P = power (watts) V = voltage (volts) I = current (amps)

Waves

	Formula	Definition of Terms
Frequency	$F = \dfrac{v}{\lambda}$	F = frequency (Hertz) v = speed (usually in m/sec) λ = wavelength (in meters)
Wavelength	$\lambda = \dfrac{v}{F}$	λ = wavelength (in meters) v = speed (usually in m/sec) F = frequency (Hertz)

Mechanical Advantage of Simple Machines

	Formula	Definition of Terms
Inclined Plane	Mechanical advantage = $\dfrac{\text{length of ramp}}{\text{height of ramp}}$	
Lever	Mechanical advantage = $\dfrac{\text{Distance}_{\text{force or effort}}}{\text{Distance}_{\text{load or resistance}}}$	$\text{Distance}_{\text{force or effort}}$ = measure of the length from the force to the fulcrum. $\text{Distance}_{\text{load or resistance}}$ = measure of the length from the fulcrum to the load.
Wheel and Axle	Mechanical advantage = $\dfrac{\text{Radius of wheel}}{\text{Radius of axle}}$	

Weight

	Formula	Definition of Terms
Weight	$W = m \cdot g_c$	W = weight (Newtons) M = mass (kilograms) g_c = 9.8 m/sec^2 (acceleration due to gravity constant)

Work

	Formula	Definition of Terms
Work	$W = F \cdot d$	W = work (watts) F = force (N) d = distance (meters)
Power	$P = \dfrac{W}{t}$	P = power (watts) W = work (watts) t = time (seconds)

Handy Tables and Charts

Quick Conversions

Distance			
Metric to Metric	Metric to Standard	Standard to Metric	Standard to Standard
1 kilometer = 1,000 meters	1 kilometer = 0.621 miles	1 mile = 1.6 kilometers	1 mile = 5,280 feet
1 meter = 0.001 kilometers	1 kilometer = 3,281 feet	1 mile = 1,609 meters	1 mile = 1,760 yards
1 meter = 100 centimeters	1 meter = 1.0936 yards	1 yard = 0.914 meters	1 yard = 3 feet
1 meter = 1,000 millimeters	1 meter = 3.281 feet	1 yard = 91.44 centimeters	1 foot = 12 inches
1 centimeter = 10 millimeters	1 meter = 39.37 inches	1 foot = 0.305 meters	
	1 centimeter = 0.394 inches	1 foot = 30.48 centimeters	
	1 millimeter = 0.039 inches	1 inch = 2.54 centimeters	
		1 inch = 25.4 millimeters	
Mass and Weight			
Metric to Metric	Metric to Standard	Standard to Metric	Standard to Standard
1 kilogram = 1,000 grams	1,000 kg = 1.1 tons	1 pound = 0.454 kg	1 pound = 16 ounces
1 gram = 0.001 kilograms	1 kilogram = 2.20 pounds	1 pound = 453.59 grams	
1 gram = 1,000 milligrams	1 gram = 0.035 ounces	1 ounce = 23.349 grams	

Quick Reference Guide

Volume			
Metric to Metric	Metric to Standard	Standard to Metric	Standard to Standard
1 liter = 0.001 kiloliters	1 meter^3 = 35 ft^3	1 gal = 3.784 liters	1 gallon = 8 pints
1 liter = 1,000 milliliters	1 liter = 0.264 gallons	1 quart = 0.946 liters	1 gallon = 4 quarts
1 milliliter = 1 cm^3	1 liter = 1.057 quarts	1 pint = 0.473 liters	1 quart = 2 pints
	1 liter = 2.1 pints	1 pint = 473.176 milliliters	
	1 milliliter = 0.061 in^3		
	1 milliliter = 0.03 ounces		

Area			
Metric to Metric	Metric to Standard	Standard to Metric	Standard to Standard
1 km^2 = 1,000,000 meters^2	1 km^2 = 0.4 miles^2	1 mile^2 = 2.6 km^2	1 mile^2 = 640 acres
1 meter^2 = 10,000 centimeters^2	1 meter^2 = 1.2 yards^2	1 yard^2 = 0.8 meter^2	1 yard^2 = 9 feet^2
1 cm^2 = 100 millimeters^2	1 cm^2 = 0.16 inches^2	1 feet^2 = 929.03 cm^2	1 feet^2 = 144 inches^2
		1 inch^2 = 6.451 cm^2	

Measurements and Their Units

Measurement	Unit Name	Symbol
Current	Ampere	A
Energy	Joule	J
Force	Newton	N
Frequency	Hertz	Hz
Power	Watt	W
Pressure	Pascal	Pa
Resistance	Ohm	Ω
Voltage	Volt	V
Weight	Newton	N
Work	Joule	J
Heat	Joule	J

Measurement	Common Units
Acceleration	m/sec^2, Mi/hr/sec
Density	g/cm^3, g/ml
Distance	Mm, cm, m, km
Mass	g, kg
Speed	m/sec, km/hr
Temperature	°C, °F, °K
Time	sec, hr
Volume	ml, l, cm^3
Distance in Space	AU

Quick Reference Guide

Celsius and Fahrenheit

Celsius	Fahrenheit	Celsius	Fahrenheit	Celsius	Fahrenheit
0	32.0	34	93.2	68	154.4
1	33.8	35	95.0	69	156.2
2	35.6	36	96.8	70	158.0
3	37.4	37	98.6	71	159.8
4	39.2	38	100.4	72	161.6
5	41.0	39	102.2	73	163.4
6	42.8	40	104.0	74	165.2
7	44.6	41	105.8	75	167.0
8	46.4	42	107.6	76	168.8
9	48.2	43	109.4	77	170.6
10	50.0	44	111.2	78	172.4
11	51.8	45	113.0	79	174.2
12	53.6	46	114.8	80	176.0
13	55.4	47	116.6	81	177.8
14	57.2	48	118.4	82	179.6
15	59.0	49	120.2	83	181.4
16	60.8	50	122.0	84	183.2
17	62.6	51	123.8	85	185.0
18	64.4	52	125.6	86	186.8
19	66.2	53	127.4	87	188.6
20	68.0	54	129.2	88	190.4
21	69.8	55	131.0	89	192.2
22	71.6	56	132.8	90	194.0
23	73.4	57	134.6	91	195.8
24	75.2	58	136.4	92	197.6
25	77.0	59	138.2	93	199.4
26	78.8	60	140.0	94	201.2
27	80.6	61	141.8	95	203.0
28	82.4	62	143.6	96	204.8
29	84.2	63	145.4	97	206.6
30	86.0	64	147.2	98	208.4
31	87.8	65	149.0	99	210.2
32	89.6	66	150.8	100	212.0
33	91.4	67	152.6		

Common Household Acids and Bases

Substance	pH	Classification
Hydrochloric Acid (HCl)	0	acid
Battery Acid (H_2SO_4; sulfuric acid)	1.0	acid
Lemon Juice	2.0	acid
Vinegar	2.2	acid
Apple	3.0	acid
Soda Pop	4.0	acid
Tomato	4.5	acid
Coffee	5.0	acid
Milk	6.6	acid
Pure Water	7.0	neutral
Salt Water	7.0	neutral
Human Blood	7.4	base
Baking Soda (Sodium Bicarbonate)	8.3	base
Most Laundry Detergents	10.0	base
Milk of Magnesia	10.5	base
Ammonia	11.0	base
Lime (Calcium Hydroxide)	12.4	base
Lye	13.0	base
Drain Cleaner (NaOH)	14.0	base

Quick Reference Guide

Common Household Chemicals

Common Name	Chemical Name	Common Name	Chemical Name
ammonia	ammonium hydroxide	lye or soda lye	sodium hydroxide
antacids	calcium carbonate	marble	mainly calcium carbonate
antifreeze	ethylene glycol	mercury oxide, black	mercurous oxide
asbestos	magnesium silicate	methanol	methyl alcohol
aspirin	acetylsalicylic acid	milk of lime	calcium hydroxide
baking soda	sodium bicarbonate	milk of magnesium	magnesium hydroxide
battery acid	sulfuric acid	milk of sulfur	precipitated sulfur
bicarbonate of soda	sodium hydrogen carbonate or sodium bicarbonate	muriatic acid	hydrochloric acid
black lead	graphite (carbon)	nail polish remover	acetone
bleaching powder	chlorinated lime; calcium hypochlorite	plaster of Paris	calcium sulfate
borax	sodium borate; sodium tetraborate	Prussic acid	hydrogen cyanide
brine	aqueous sodium chloride solution	quartz sand	silicon dioxide
chalk	calcium carbonate	quicksilver	mercury
corn starch	amylose	rock salt	sodium chloride
cream of tartar	potassium bitartrate	rubbing alcohol	isopropyl alcohol
dextrose	glucose	soda water	carbonic acid
diamond	carbon crystal	table salt	sodium chloride
dry ice	carbon dioxide	table sugar	sucrose
Epsom salts	magnesium sulfate	talc or talcum	magnesium silicate
glycerin	glycerol	vinegar	impure diluted acetic acid
gypsum	natural calcium sulfate	vitamin C	ascorbic acid
household bleach	sodium hypochlorite	washing soda	sodium carbonate
laughing gas	nitrous oxide		
lime	calcium oxide		
limewater	solution of calcium hydroxide		
lite salt	potassium chloride		

Periodic Table

No.	Symbol	Atomic Mass	Name
1	H	1.00794	Hydrogen
2	He	4.002602	Helium
3	Li	6.941	Lithium
4	Be	9.012182	Beryllium
5	B	10.811	Boron
6	C	12.0107	Carbon
7	N	14.0067	Nitrogen
8	O	15.9994	Oxygen
9	F	18.9984032	Fluorine
10	Ne	20.1797	Neon
11	Na	22.989769	Sodium
12	Mg	24.3050	Magnesium
13	Al	26.9815386	Aluminium
14	Si	28.0855	Silicon
15	P	30.973762	Phosphorus
16	S	32.065	Sulfur
17	Cl	35.453	Chlorine
18	Ar	39.948	Argon
19	K	39.0983	Potassium
20	Ca	40.078	Calcium
21	Sc	44.955912	Scandium
22	Ti	47.867	Titanium
23	V	50.9415	Vanadium
24	Cr	51.9961	Chromium
25	Mn	54.938045	Manganese
26	Fe	55.845	Iron
27	Co	58.933195	Cobalt
28	Ni	58.6934	Nickel
29	Cu	63.546	Copper
30	Zn	65.38	Zinc
31	Ga	69.723	Gallium
32	Ge	72.64	Germanium
33	As	74.92160	Arsenic
34	Se	78.96	Selenium
35	Br	79.904	Bromine
36	Kr	83.798	Krypton
37	Rb	85.4678	Rubidium
38	Sr	87.62	Strontium
39	Y	88.90585	Yttrium
40	Zr	91.224	Zirconium
41	Nb	92.90638	Niobium
42	Mo	95.96	Molybdenum
43	Tc	[98]	Technetium
44	Ru	101.07	Ruthenium
45	Rh	102.90550	Rhodium
46	Pd	106.42	Palladium
47	Ag	107.8682	Silver
48	Cd	112.411	Cadmium
49	In	114.818	Indium
50	Sn	118.710	Tin
51	Sb	121.760	Antimony
52	Te	127.60	Tellurium
53	I	126.90447	Iodine
54	Xe	131.293	Xenon
55	Cs	132.9054519	Cesium
56	Ba	137.327	Barium
57	La	138.90547	Lanthanum
58	Ce	140.116	Cerium
59	Pr	140.90765	Praseodymium
60	Nd	144.242	Neodymium
61	Pm	[145]	Promethium
62	Sm	150.36	Samarium
63	Eu	151.964	Europium
64	Gd	157.25	Gadolinium
65	Tb	158.92535	Terbium
66	Dy	162.500	Dysprosium
67	Ho	164.93032	Holmium
68	Er	167.259	Erbium
69	Tm	168.93421	Thulium
70	Yb	173.054	Ytterbium
71	Lu	174.9668	Lutetium
72	Hf	178.49	Hafnium
73	Ta	180.94788	Tantalum
74	W	183.84	Tungsten
75	Re	186.207	Rhenium
76	Os	190.23	Osmium
77	Ir	192.217	Iridium
78	Pt	195.084	Platinum
79	Au	196.966569	Gold
80	Hg	200.59	Mercury
81	Tl	204.3833	Thallium
82	Pb	207.2	Lead
83	Bi	208.98040	Bismuth
84	Po	[209]	Polonium
85	At	[210]	Astatine
86	Rn	[222]	Radon
87	Fr	[223]	Francium
88	Ra	[226]	Radium
89	Ac	[227]	Actinium
90	Th	232.03806	Thorium
91	Pa	231.03588	Protactinium
92	U	238.02891	Uranium
93	Np	[237]	Neptunium
94	Pu	[244]	Plutonium
95	Am	[243]	Americium
96	Cm	[247]	Curium
97	Bk	[247]	Berkelium
98	Cf	[251]	Californium
99	Es	[252]	Einsteinium
100	Fm	[257]	Fermium
101	Md	[258]	Mendelevium
102	No	[259]	Nobelium
103	Lr	[262]	Lawrencium
104	Rf	[267]	Rutherfordium
105	Db	[268]	Dubnium
106	Sg	[271]	Seaborgium
107	Bh	[272]	Bohrium
108	Hs	[270]	Hassium
109	Mt	[276]	Meitnerium
110	Ds	[281]	Darmstadtium
111	Rg	[280]	Roentgenium
112	Uub	[285]	Ununbium
113	Uut	[284]	Ununtrium
114	Uuq	[289]	Ununquadium
115	Uup	[288]	Ununpentium
116	Uuh	[293]	Ununhexium
117	Uus	[294]	Ununseptium
118	Uuo	[294]	Ununoctium

Group labels (top): 1A, 2A, 3B, 4B, 5B, 6B, 7B, 8B, 1B, 2B, 3A, 4A, 5A, 6A, 7A, 8A

Lanthanides: 57–71
Actinides: 89–103

Legend: Alkali Metals · Alkaline Earth Metals · Transition Metals · Rare Earth Metals · Other Metals · Metalloids · Non-metals · Halogens · Noble Gases

Basic Weather Map Symbols

Cloud Coverage

○ No Clouds
◑ Partly Cloudy
● Overcast

Wind Direction

Wind comes from the direction of the arrow.

Misc. Sky Cover

⸗ Patchy Fog
= Light Fog
≡ Dense Fog

Air Pressure

H High
L Low

Cloud Types

High Elevation

⌐ Scattered Cirrus
⌐⟩ Dense Cirrus
⌐(Cirrostratus
)⌐(Heavy Cirrostratus
⌐) Cirrus and Cirrostratus

Middle Elevation

／ Thin Altostratus
⫽ Thick Altostratus
⌇ Thin Altocumulus
⟅ Heavy Altocumulus

Low Elevation

⌄ Stratocumulus
⌒ Fair Weather Cumulus
⌂ Developing Cumulus
⌂ Cumulonimbus
∿ Cirrocumulus
⫽ Nimbostratus
— Stratus

Weather Conditions

	Light	Moderate	Heavy
Rain	•	•	•
Snow	*	*	*
Drizzle	,	,	,

Steady

	Light	Moderate	Heavy
Rain	••	••	••
Snow	**	**	**
Drizzle	,,	,,	,,

Wind Speed

◎ Calm
—— < 5 knots
—⟍ 5 knots
—⟍ 10 knots
—⟍ 20 knots
—⟍ 25 knots
—◣ 50 knots

Fronts

Warm
(usually red)

Cold
(usually blue)

Stationary
(mix of red and blue)

Occluded
(mix of red and blue)

Lunar Phases

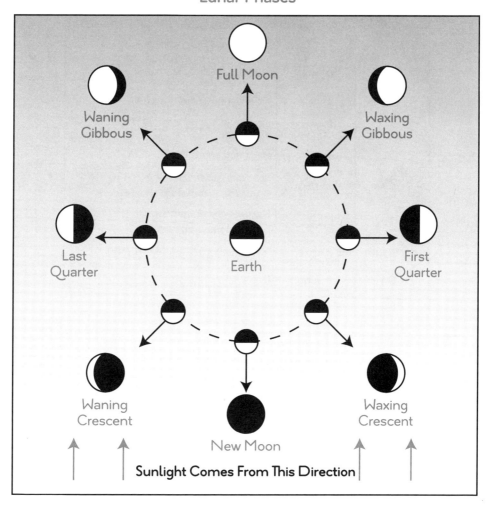

Moh's Hardness Scale

Hardness	Mineral	Description
1	Talc	Fingernail scratches it easily.
2	Gypsum	Fingernail scratches it.
3	Calcite	Copper penny scratches it.
4	Fluorite	Steel nail scratches it easily.
5	Apatite	Steel nail scratches it.
6	Feldspar	Steel nail does not scratch it easily, but the mineral scratches glass.
7	Quartz	Hardest common mineral. It scratches a steel nail and glass easily.
8	Topaz	Harder than any common mineral.
9	Corundum	It scratches topaz.
10	Diamond	Scratches all other minerals.

Quick Reference Guide

Geologic Timeline

Era	Period	Million Years Ago	Characteristic Life
Cenozoic	Quaternary	1.8	Birth of modern plants, animals, and man. Humans existed during the last 5–8 million years. Ice ages begin and end.
Cenozoic	Tertiary	65	"The Age of the Mammals": Modern whales and large mammals begin to appear including horses, dogs, and bears.
Mesozoic	Cretaceous	146	"The Age of the Dinosaur": Extinction of reptile-like birds and many other reptiles by the end of this period. Dinosaurs are dwindling. Continents are located very much as they are now.
Mesozoic	Jurassic	208	First reptilian birds. Reptiles can be found in almost all habitats and biomes. Climate was warm all year round.
Mesozoic	Triassic	247	Pangaea broke apart. Earliest dinosaurs, flying reptiles, and marine reptiles existed. Primitive mammals appeared. Warm climate.
Paleozoic	Permian	280	"The Age of Amphibian": Primitive reptiles. Because of the change in climate from cold at the beginning to warm, a lot of species became extinct by the end. Pangaea exists.
Paleozoic	Pennsylvanian	330	Insects on the rise. Reptiles first appear. Climate warm and humid. The first cockroaches appear.
Paleozoic	Mississippian	360	Extinction of some fish species, which others diversified. Amphibians began to diversify. Plants die and begin to form present-day coal. First winged insects.
Paleozoic	Devonian	408	"The Age of the Fishes": Lots of fish, although many jawless varieties began to disappear.
Paleozoic	Silurian	438	Earliest known land animals. Primitive plants. Rise of fishes.
Paleozoic	Ordovician	505	Vertebrates appear with primitive plants. Trilobites and cephalopods abundant.
Paleozoic	Cambrian	540–500	"Age of the Trilobites": Lots of shallow seas. Earliest shellfish. Trilobites are common.
Precambrian	Proterozoic	2,500	Primitive plants and animals in the ocean. Changes in the Earth's crust produced major landmasses.
Precambrian	Archeozoic or Archean	4,600	Formation of the Earth and slow development of the lithosphere, hydrosphere, and atmosphere. Development of sea life. Oldest known life (known through fossil records).

Note. From Geology.com (n.d.), Hyperphysics (n.d.)., & U.S. Geological Survey (2002).

References

Geology.com. (n.d.). *Geologic time scale*. Retrieved March 9, 2009, from
http://geology.com/time.htm

Hyperphyics. (n.d.). *Geological time scale*. Retrieved March 9, 2009, from
http://hyperphysics.phy-astr.gsu.edu/Hbase/Geophys/geotime.html

U.S. Geological Survey. (2006). *Geologic history of Southern California*.
Retrieved March 9, 2009, from http://geomaps.wr.usgs.gov/socal/
geology/geologic_history/index.html

U

Unsaturated Solution 57

V

Vacuole 21, 34
Valence Electrons 57
Vertebrate 35
Volt (V) 17, 119
Voltage 58, 119
  Formula for 115
Volume 58, 119
  Measuring 92
  Quick Conversions 118

W

Waning 125
Warm-Blooded 35
Water Cycle 75
Watts (W) 18, 119
Wavelength 58
  Formula for 58, 115
Waxing 125
Weathering 76
  Chemical 61
  Physical or Mechanical 71
Weather Map Symbols 75, 124
Wedge 59
Weight 59, 119
  Formula for 116
  Quick Conversions 117
Wheel and Axle 59
  Calculating the Mechanical
    Advantage of 59, 116
White Dwarf 85
Wind Power 76
Work 59, 119
  Formulas for 59, 116
  to Calculate Power 52

X

Xylem 35

Z

Zygote 35

About the Author

After teaching science for more than 15 years, both overseas and in the U.S., Laurie E. Westphal now works as an independent gifted education and science consultant. She enjoys developing and presenting staff development on differentiation for various districts and conferences, working with teachers to assist them in planning and developing lessons to meet the needs of their advanced students.

Laurie currently resides in Houston, TX, and has made it her goal to share her vision for real-world, product-based lessons that help all students become critical thinkers and effective problem solvers. She is the author of the *Differentiating Instruction With Menus* series as well as *Hands-On Physical Science*.